BLUEPRINT FOR A
GREEN ECONOMY

BLUEPRINT FOR A GREEN ECONOMY

a report by
David Pearce
Anil Markandya
Edward B. Barbier *of*
The London Environmental Economics Centre

for
The UK Department of the Environment

Earthscan Publications Ltd   LONDON

First published in 1989 by
Earthscan Publications Limited
120 Pentonville Road, London N1 9JN

Sixth printing 1992

First printed in this format 1994
Reprinted 1996, 1997 and 1999

British Library Cataloguing in Publication Data
Pearce, David
    Blueprint for a green economy.
    1. Great Britain. Environment. Pollution. Control measures.
    Economic aspects.
    I. Title   II. Markandya, Anil   III. Barbier, Edward B.   IV. London
    Environmental Economics Centre   V. Great Britain,
    Department of the Environment
    338.4'76285'0941

ISBN 1-85383-066-6

Original cover design by David King
Production by David Williams Associates
Typeset by Rapid Communications Ltd, London WC1
Printed and bound in Great Britain by
Biddles Ltd, Guildford and King's Lynn

Earthscan Publications Limited is an editorially independent subsidary of
Kogan Page Limited, and publishes in association with the International Institute
for Environment and Development and the World Wide Fund for Nature.

FOREWORD

This book was originally prepared as a report for the Department of the Environment in the United Kingdom under research contract 7/8/131 "Sustainable Development, Resource Accounting and Project Appraisal: State of the Art Review". It was released to the London Environmental Economics Centre (LEEC) for publication in August 1989. LEEC is a joint venture, established in 1988, by the International Institute for Environment and Development (IIED) and the Department of Economics of University College, London (UCL).

The views expressed in this book are those of the authors and must not be taken as reflecting the views of the Department of the Environment.

The authors wish to thank Peter MacCormack and John Corkindale of the Department of the Environment for detailed comments on an earlier draft; Joanne Burgess and Sue Pearce for invaluable research assistance; countless organizations and individuals for supplying information; and the staff of Earthscan for enthusiastic support in publishing the report in record time.

David W. Pearce, Professor of Economics at UCL and Director of LEEC.
Dr Anil Markandya, Senior Lecturer in Economics at UCL and Associate Director of LEEC.
Dr Edward B. Barbier, Associate Director of LEEC.

CONTENTS

"Where are the lollipops in sustainable development?"
Canadian politician, 1988.

PREFACE

In 1987 the World Commission on Environment and Development (WCED: the "Brundtland Commission") published *Our Common Future*. The Brundtland Report firmly established the concept of *sustainable development* as the basis for an integrative approach to economic policy in the coming decades. The WCED was created by the United Nations as a result of a General Assembly resolution in autumn 1985. It was the third in a series of UN initiatives. The first manifested itself in the Brandt Commission's *Programme for Survival* and *Common Crisis*. The second was the Palme Commission's work on security and disarmament, *Common Security*.

There were precursors to the Brundtland Commission. The *World Conservation Strategy* of 1980 (IUCN, 1980) had already advanced the idea of sustainable development and had recognized the challenge of integrating development and environment:

> Development and conservation are equally necessary for our survival and for the discharge of our responsibilities as trustees of natural resources for the generations to come. (IUCN, 1980, p.1)

But the World Conservation Strategy did not succeed in integrating economics with environment: it did not show what conservation might mean for economic policy, or how misguided economic policy could degrade the environment, or how better economic policy could act as a major force to improve the environment. These omissions perhaps reflected the state of play at the time. But things have changed. The world has become "greener" (see Box 0.1) and our understanding of the

Box 0.1 **The political importance of environment in the European Community**

VERY IMPORTANT POLITICAL PROBLEMS TODAY (1988)

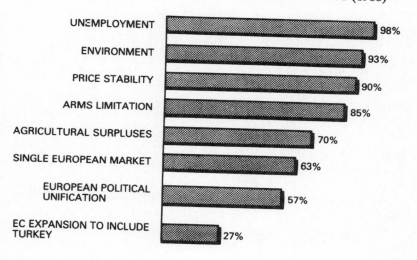

Those who reply only: don't know/no answer vary from 1% to 4% from item to item.

Within the European Community, the environment ranks as the second most important political problem perceived by the electorate, ahead of inflation and arms control, and second only to unemployment.

Source: DG Information, Communication and Culture, Brussels, *Eurobarometer*, No. 30, December 1988.

environment–economy interaction advances day by day.[1]

The message of the Brundtland Report was that it is *possible* to achieve a path of economic development for the global economy which meets the needs of the present generation *without* compromising the chances of future generations to meet their needs. At the risk of oversimplification, the prescription is to leave to future generations a *wealth* inheritance – a stock of knowledge and understanding, a stock of technology, a stock of man-made capital *and* a stock of environmental assets – no less than that inherited by the current generation. As the Brundtland Commission put it:

> Humanity has the ability to make development sustainable – to ensure that it meets the needs of the present without compromising the ability of future generations to meet their own needs. (WCED, 1987, p.8)

No definition is ever satisfactorily "tight" and the Brundtland Report is not consistent throughout its text as to what it means by sustainable development. But the search for precise meanings is not the subject of the current report: *we are concerned to investigate some of the economic underpinnings of the idea of sustainable development: to ask, in other words, whether economics throws light on the meaning of sustainable development and whether it is a feasible, practical concept.*

We argue that the answers to both these questions is "yes".

● Economics throws light on the meaning of sustainable development because the environment and the economy *necessarily interact.* Economic systems impact on the environment by using up resources, by emitting waste products to receiving environmental media, by changing the aesthetic functions of natural and built environments, and – constituting the "new" environmental challenge for the twenty-first century – by altering the global life-support systems on which we all depend.

● Sustainable development is feasible. It requires a shift in the *balance* of the way economic progress is pursued. Environmental concerns must be properly integrated into economic policy from the highest (macroeconomic) level to the most detailed (microeconomic) level. The environment must be seen as a valuable, frequently essential input to human wellbeing. Sustainable development means a change in *consumption* patterns towards environmentally more benign products, and a change in *investment* patterns towards augmenting environmental capital.

If we accept sustainable development as a working idea, what might it mean for the way we manage a modern economy? This is the second major feature of this report. Our terms of reference ask us to "review the state of the art on the relationship between the sustainable development concept, national accounting, resource accounting, satellite accounting, and project appraisal procedures" (T.O.R, para.4).

We show that sustainable development *does* have implications for the way in which we record economic progress (the "accounting" framework). We show that it does affect project appraisal – i.e. the way in which we think about capital investments in the UK and how we might re-evaluate the loans given for foreign capital investment (overseas aid). We also dwell on some of the implications implicit in the terms of reference. It is not possible to evaluate the implications for project appraisal, for example, without saying something about what sustainable development means for the *pricing* of inputs, goods and services in a free market economy. Nor can we ignore the difficult issue of how to weigh up the relative balance of gains and losses between the present and the future – the *intergenerational question*.

Finally, we place the whole discussion in the context of environmental policy, and UK environmental policy in particular. The justification for this is that the underlying theme of the Brundtland Commission, simply put, is that environmental policy matters not just for the quality of life in general, not just because natural environments have values "in themselves", but because environments and economies are not distinct. Treating them as if they were is the surest recipe for unsustainable development.

The current report can be seen as a logical outcome of the UK government's initial response to the Brundtland Report where it is stated:

the UK fully intends to continue building on this approach [environmental improvement] and further to develop policies consistent with the concept of *sustainable development*.[2]

We hope the current report assists that process. We would like to think, too, that our findings are of relevance to other countries seeking to ensure sustainable development for the future.

Notes

1. It is significant that the second World Conservation Strategy (WCS), *Managing for the Future*, is now under preparation (1989). The London Environmental Economics Centre is actively participating in the preparation of the economics "input" to WCS II.
2. UK Government, *Our Common Future: a Perspective by the United Kingdom on the Report of the World Commission on Environment and Development*, London, July 1988.

1. INTRODUCTION

The idea of sustainable development

In the last decade a central concept in the debate about future economic progress, nationally, internationally and globally, has been "sustainable development". Definitions of sustainable development abound. There is some truth in the criticism that it has come to mean whatever suits the particular advocacy of the individual concerned. This is not surprising. It is difficult to be against "sustainable development". It sounds like something we should all approve of, like "motherhood and apple pie". But what constitutes development, or progress, for one person may not be development or progress for another. "Development" is a "value word": it embodies personal ideals and aspirations and concepts of what constitutes the "good" society (see Chapter 2).

Yet, in all the writing on sustainable development there is a common thread, a fairly consistent set of characteristics that appear to define the conditions for sustainable development to be achieved.

The term "sustainable development" itself ought not to occasion much controversy. Development is some set of desirable goals or objectives for society. Those goals undoubtedly include the basic aim to secure a rising level of real income per capita – what is traditionally regarded as the "standard of living". But most people would also now accept that there is more to development than rising real incomes – "economic growth". There is now an emphasis on the "quality of life", on the health of the population, on educational standards and general social wellbeing.

Sustainable development involves devising a social and

economic system which ensures that these goals are sustained, i.e. that real incomes rise, that educational standards increase, that the health of the nation improves, that the general quality of life is advanced.

The means of achieving sustainable development in this broad sense might be summarized as follows:

The value of the environment
● Sustainable development involves a substantially increased emphasis on the value of natural, built and cultural environments. This "higher profile" arises either because environmental quality is seen as an increasingly important factor contributing to the achievement of "traditional" development objectives such as rising real incomes, or simply because environmental quality is part of the wider development objective of an improved "quality of life".

Extending the time horizon
● Sustainable development involves a concern both with the short- to medium-term horizons, say the 5 to 10 years over which a political party might plan and implement its manifesto, *and* with the longer-run future to be inherited by our grandchildren, and perhaps beyond.

Equity
● Sustainable development places emphasis on providing for the needs of the least advantaged in society ("intragenerational equity"), and on a fair treatment of future generations ("intergenerational equity").

Chapter 2 elaborates on these three key characteristics and explains why increased emphasis on them is thought to make the process of economic change more sustainable, more lasting.

Annex 1 (p. 172) quotes various definitions of sustainable development and shows how they have the common features of the three key concepts: *environment, futurity* and *equity*.

These three concepts of environment, futurity and equity are integrated in sustainable development through a general underlying theme. This theme is that *future generations should be compensated for reductions in the endowments of resources brought about by the actions of present generations*.

The underlying logic of this proposition is in fact very simple. If one generation leaves the next generation with less wealth then it has made the future worse off. But sustainable development is about making people better off. Hence a policy which leaves more wealth for future development.

Sustainable development as a bequest to the future

The way in which this compensation should take place is at the heart of the debate over sustainable development. Two broad views may be discerned:

(i) compensation for the future is best achieved by ensuring that current generations leave the succeeding generations with at least as much capital wealth as the current generation inherited;

(ii) compensation for the future should be focused not only on man-made capital wealth, but should pay special attention to environmental wealth. That is, future generations must not inherit less environmental capital than the current generation inherited.

Notice that a distinction is being made between two types of capital, or wealth. The first is the wealth with which we are all familiar – *capital wealth*. This is the stock of all man-made things such as roads and factories, computers and human intelligence. The other form of wealth is *natural* wealth or natural capital. This comprises the stock of environmentally given assets such as soil and forest, wildlife and water. The two types of capital are not wholly distinct: humans plant forests and breed animals, for example. But the distinction is helpful in understanding what it means when we talk of "environment and economy", and it become especially important when we look at how the future is to be compensated by the past for losses of natural capital.

The distinction between the two points of view about how

to compensate the future is important. For the first allows any generation to degrade natural environments *provided* man-made capital wealth is substituted for it. The second view does not dispute the importance of wealth creation in this sense, but it insists on the special importance of environmental wealth, the stock of natural assets.

Economy and environment

The philosophy of sustainable development borrows freely from the science of *environmental economics* in several major respects. A basic aspect of environmental economics concerns our understanding of the ways in which economies and their environments interact.

Fundamental to an understanding of sustainable development is the fact that the economy is *not separate from the environment in which we live*. There is an interdependence both because the way we manage the economy impacts on the environment, *and* because environmental quality impacts on the performance of the economy.

The former type of interaction is familiar to most people. The latter, perhaps, is not.

The risks of treating economic management and environmental quality *as if* they are separate, non-interacting elements have now become apparent. The world could not have continued to use chlorofluorocarbons (CFCs) indiscriminately. That use was, and is, affecting the ozone layer. In turn, damage to the ozone layer affects human health and economic productivity. Few would argue now that we can perpetually postpone taking action to contain the emission of greenhouse gases (GHGs). Our use of fossil fuels is driven by the goals of economic change, and that process will affect global climate. In turn, climate warming and sea-level rise will affect the performance of economies.

This *two-way interaction* is absolutely fundamental to sustainable development thinking. Economies affect environments. Environments affect economies.

The fact that economies and environments interact, and the fact that economic policy devoid of concern for the environment risks both environmental stress and economic damage, may not matter much. We have first to establish that the environmental losses are significant in themselves or that their impact on the economy is significant. Second, even if these impacts are significant, it may pay us to do little about it until later. A problem postponed may be better than a problem tackled now if only because costs incurred later on are preferable to costs incurred now.[1] The two issues being raised here are:

- the value of the environment, and
- the costs and benefits of *anticipatory policy*.

We address each issue in turn:

Valuing the environment

One of the central themes of environmental economics, and central to sustainable development thinking also, is the need to place proper values on the services provided by natural environments. The central problem is that many of these services are provided "free". They have a zero price simply because no market place exists in which their true values can be revealed through the acts of buying and selling. Examples might be a fine view, the water purification and storm protection functions of coastal wetlands, or the biological diversity within a tropical forest. The elementary theory of supply and demand tells us that if something is provided at a zero price, more of it will be demanded than if there was a positive price. Very simply, the cheaper it is the more will be demanded. The danger is that this greater level of demand will be unrelated to the capacity of the relevant natural environments to meet the demand. For example, by treating the ozone layer as a resource with a zero price there never was any incentive to protect it. Its value to human populations and to the global environment in general did not show up anywhere in a balance sheet of profit or loss, or of costs and benefits.

The important principle is that resources and environments serve economic functions and have positive economic value. To

Box 1.1   **Environmental problems arising from the absence of markets**

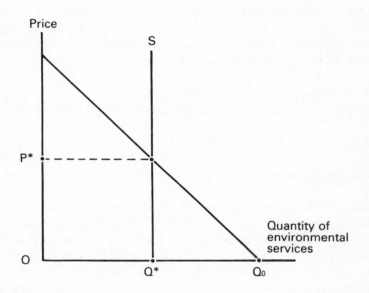

The diagram shows the demand, D, for the services of a natural environment. If there was a price, the demand would be greater the lower the price (imagine an entrance fee to a national park, for example). The supply is generally fixed, however. This is shown by the vertical supply curve, S. If there was a market in the environment in question, price would settle at P^* – the "equilibrium price" – and the amount of the environment used up would be Q^*. But, in fact, the absence of a market in the environment means that the price is zero and the quantity consumed is Q_0. "Too much" of the environment is consumed. This is sufficient to establish the importance of valuing the economic functions of environments. We also need to ask how we can be sure that even a price P^* will prevent the environment from being degraded over time.

treat them as if they had zero value is seriously to risk overusing the resource. An "economic function" in this context is any service that contributes to human well-being, to the "standard of living", or "development". *This simple logic underlines the importance of valuing the environment correctly and integrating those correct values into economic policy.*

It is this argument that leads us to reject the first line of reasoning against the emphasis on environmental quality. We have a sound *a priori* case for supposing that the environment has been used to excess. Its degradation results, in part at least, from the fact that it is treated as a zero-priced resource when, in fact, it serves economic functions that have positive value.

Notice that this does not mean we should automatically introduce actual, positive prices for environmental functions wherever we can. There is a case for "making the user pay", as we shall see. But for the moment the important principle to establish is that in our economic accounting, in the weighing up of the pros and cons of capital investments and economic policies, we should try, as best we can, to record the economic values that natural environments provide. It is, after all, something of an accident that some goods and services and some natural resources have markets whereas others do not. Even if it is possible to argue that, eventually, all natural resources will generate their own markets,[2] we have no assurance at all that those markets will evolve before the resource is extinguished or irreparably damaged.

Box 1.1 illustrates the idea that a zero-priced resource will be "overused" in economic terms.

Anticipatory and reactive environmental policy

A second reason was advanced as to why we may not have to worry about elevating environmental issues to matters of major concern: we may always be able to postpone taking action. One reason for postponing action is that future costs are less burdensome than current costs. This reflects what economists call "time preference" or "discounting the future". Simply put, we all possess a degree of impatience. We would rather that the new car arrived tomorrow than wait for it for a year. We would prefer our wages or salary now than wait until the end of the week or the month. In a society which is based on letting people's preferences count, as market-based economies are, it is not logical to accept the role those preferences play in the allocation of goods within society *now*, while rejecting the preferences that people have for the present over the future.

Respecting time preference is just as much a feature of "consumer sovereignty" as respecting people's rights to buy and sell what they choose in the market place. The issue is much more complex than this, as Chapter 6 shows. But if we at least acknowledge the existence of time preference, we will have to accept that postponing problems is a sound policy *in so far as this one criterion is concerned*.

It *may* therefore make sense not to act precipitately about an environmental problem such as climate change. After all, policies undertaken to deal with climate change problems are likely to be expensive, or at least more expensive than traditional environmental policy has been. We might say that it sometimes makes sense to behave in the *reactive mode* for environmental policy. This contrasts with the *anticipatory mode* in which we try to anticipate problems and incur the costs of solving the problem in advance of the problem occurring.

The issue of time preference is, however, only one aspect of the problem of choosing between anticipatory and reactive environmental policy. At least four other issues affect any choice between these policy stances.

First, by postponing a policy we cannot be sure that it will cost the same to solve it in the future as it would cost if action was taken now. Indeed, for many problems it is highly likely that it will cost more. A particular extreme instance of such rising costs occurs when the damage done by delay is *irreversible*. For example, suppose that nothing at all had been done about the damage to the ozone layer from trace gases. There are no (feasible) technologies for reconstituting the layer once it is "holed". The damage done, for example through the contribution to climate warming, is irreversible. One way of thinking about irreversibility is to say that it would cost virtually infinite sums to correct the damage. Another, perhaps less dramatic view, is to say that we have to tolerate whatever the irreversible damage is for a very long time, perhaps for ever.

The rising cost of reactive policy, particularly where irreversible effects are concerned, could easily offset the effect of time preference (discounting).

Second, the reactive stance may not be compatible with the underlying theme of sustainable development. Recall that the sustainable development idea was encapsulated in the proposition that the future has to be compensated by the past. Otherwise the future will be worse off than the present and the resulting development is not sustainable.[3] Undertaking reactive policy toward the environment could, as noted above, result in irreversible cost to the future. The potential for irreversibility is thus sufficient for us to be highly suspect of reactive policy: it should be undertaken only if we can be sure that damage can be reversed and at a cost that can be "afforded" by the future. What the future can afford depends on what we leave them by way of inherited wealth, natural and man-made.

The philosophy of sustainable development tends to favour strongly the anticipatory approach to environmental policy.

Third, the reactive stance receives some support from a not always appreciated fact. This is that delay can generate better information which in turn enables cheaper and more effective solutions in the future. The implicit condition here is that the delay is accompanied by further research aimed at such cost-effective solutions. If delay is adopted simply to postpone costs without any associated research activity, then this benefit is lost.

Reactive policy is not wholly bad. It can sometimes be justified by reference to the expected gains in information and improved policy cost-effectiveness. But delay is only justified if the benefits outweigh the costs: good scientific research needs to accompany delay.

Fourth, we have the problem of *uncertainty*. Environmental problems are often treated as if they are some minor deviation in the working of an economic system. But the most essential feature about environments is that their workings are *pervasive* in the economic system. This pervasiveness arises from the simple fact that all economic activity uses up materials and resources and requires energy, and these, in turn, must end up somewhere – in dumps, dissipated in the atmosphere, disposed of to the oceans or whatever. This pervasiveness might not be unduly troublesome but for the fact that it contributes to the uncertainty about how environmental impacts will manifest themselves. A toxic pollutant disposed of at point A may travel to point B miles away. In the process it may mix with other pollutants and the damage from the combined effect may be greater than the sum of the damages from the individual effects ("synergism"). To these kinds of uncertainties must be added the scientific uncertainty about how ecosystems function – consider the fact that we are some way away from understanding how global carbon cycles work in detail and hence how climate change will impact regionally within the world.

How then should we behave under uncertainty? Attitudes to uncertainty vary. There are, for example, technological optimists who believe that whatever problem is generated there will be some technological solution. Such optimism is the stuff of scientific advance and we would all be the poorer (some might disagree) but for it. The problem is one of what happens if the optimists are not right and we behave *as if* they were. Box 1.2 shows how we might (simplistically) present such choices. What it reveals is that the cost of pursuing an optimist policy could be disastrous if in fact some form of "prudent pessimism" turns out to be right. Prudent pessimism might well deprive society of some moderate gains (and we argue shortly that the losses are only likely to be moderate) and, if the optimists turn out to be right all along, then we will have sacrificed the difference between high and moderate gains.

There are really no rules for choosing which policy to undertake in the face of uncertainty. But most people are risk-averse, they do not like uncertainty. Most people would also agree that taking risks is not worthwhile when the negative "pay-off" – what happens if they lose – is very large. Some current environmental problems risk very large losses.[4] A risk-averse strategy favours

Box 1.2 **A "pay-off matrix" for approaches to environmental uncertainty**

		Actual state of the world	
		Optimists right	Pessimists right
Type of policy	Optimistic	HIGH	DISASTER
	Pessimistic	MODERATE	TOLERABLE

The pay-off matrix suggests that if the technological optimists are right and a policy of relative indifference to the environment is pursued, then society might make high gains. If the optimistic policy is pursued and the pessimists turn out to be right then some form of "disaster" might occur. Pursuit of "prudent pessimism" on the other hand results in moderate gains or, at worst, tolerable gains. The terminology is suggestive only, of course. Substituting "nirvana" for "high" might alter the perception of the matrix a little! None the less, the basic idea of seeing what happens if a given policy is pursued, when in fact the state of the world is not consistent with that policy, is correct.

The matrix is adapted from Robert Costanza, "What is Ecological Economics?", *Ecological Economics*, Vol.1, no.1, 1989, pp.1–7.

anticipatory and not reactive environmental policy.

The challenge of global pollution

If there is anything "new" about the environmental challenges of the closing twentieth century it is that they, increasingly, are international, global and potentially more life-threatening than in the past. Global pollution in the form of damage to the ozone layer, and damage from global warming and sea-level rise due to greenhouse gases, is of particular concern.

Global pollution presents a special challenge for several reasons. If its worst effects are realized, then some countries will experience catastrophic damage. No one country acting alone can do much to prevent or contain these impacts: only a coalition of governments worldwide can do this. Yet the costs of such a coalition are high in terms of changes to consumption and investment patterns, and the uncertainty of the effects of global pollution may well inhibit individual countries from joining a worldwide coalition. Some countries may even gain from some aspects of global warming: they may have even less incentive to cooperate. *Perversely, the global challenge is that world cooperation might be least likely in a context where the world stands to lose the most.*

The essential problem is that the atmosphere and stratosphere are *global open access*: they are shared by all nations without any restrictions being in place to police or restrict the use of the resource. Much the same is true for the world's oceans. Some parts of the ocean are *common property* resources: access to them is restricted to a "club" of users, maybe a nation's fishing fleet, or several nations' fleets. Environmental economics predicts that common property resources run the *risk* of over-use, while open access resources are *very* likely to be overused, especially as population grows and as economic demands on these environments increase. Put another way, the benefits of these resources are *public goods* – once the functions of the biosphere and its global sinks are provided to one nation they are provided to all, and there is no mechanism for "excluding" nations from these benefits.

Global warming and sea-level rise from the "greenhouse effect" illustrate the discussion about anticipatory and reactive environmental policy. It is tempting to think that because the impacts of the greenhouse effect are some way into the future (although some recent climatic events *may* be associated with warming that has already occurred) we can safely delay taking action. Certainly, there is no question that substantial additional scientific research needs to be undertaken before

Box 1.3 **Relative contributions of greenhouse gases**

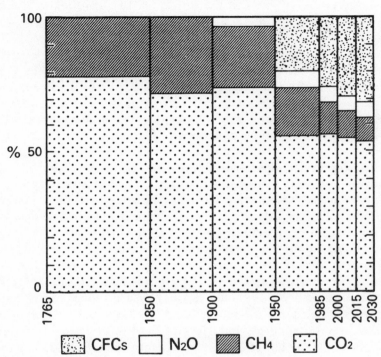

Source: T. Wigley, "Relative contributions of different trade gases to the greenhouse effect", *Climate Monitor*, Vol.16, 1987.

the most carefully designed policies can be applied.

To see this, consider the types of uncertainty that exist.

i) *Uncertainty about trace gas emissions.* Box 1.3 summarizes the types of gases contributing to the "greenhouse effect", and the relative contributions of each type, both historically and prospectively. It is clear that the future warming, beyond that to which the earth is already committed, will arise mainly from CO_2 and CFC emissions. It follows that part of the uncertainty about global warming will arise from uncertainty about the future fuel mix. This will take in such variables as the role of energy conservation and the impact of the Montreal/Helsinki Protocol on CFCs.

(ii) *Uncertainty about climate response.* How the climate responds to the "doses" of trace gases is itself uncertain. This reflects scientific uncertainty about the processes involved, and the varying degrees of complexity in global climate models. Recent work on the role of cloud cover and its effects on warming illustrate the problems.

(iii) *Regional impact uncertainty.* Uncertainty about the regional climate response is greater than that attached to the mean global temperature increase. Existing global circulation models (GCMs) do not yet have the capacity to predict regional climate change: the finest grid spacing in current models relates to an area about the size of France.

(iv) *Threshold uncertainty.* A further issue relates to the existence of thresholds for some of the physical impacts of climate change. The most obvious case is sea-level rise. Rises of X cms may not matter, but rises of X + 1 cms might. Given the uncertainty about the rate of climate change and hence the rate of sea-level rise, it is uncertain as to *when* such impacts will occur. The "snapshot" approach, whereby a particular year is targeted in terms of assessing impacts, could thus be misleading. An impact that does not occur in 2030, say, cannot be assumed to be only marginally worse in 2035: it may be associated with the passing of a threshold. There is high potential for "surprises" in climatic change.

(v) *Uncertainty about social response.* There are two major sources of uncertainty relating to the way in which societies will respond to climate change. These are:
1) the degree of "natural adaptation" that will occur; and
2) the degree of governmental policy response that will occur.

Natural adaptation

Much climatic change will have "gradual" impacts. It must be supposed that there will be an extensive amount of ongoing adaptation undertaken by individuals and communities independently of significant policy interventions by governments. This type of adaptation could include such phenomena as:

● population migrations;
● alterations in lifestyle (e.g. changes in consumption patterns, or travel modes); or
● undertaking "defensive expenditures" (e.g. increased use of fertilizers to maintain existing farm productivity levels).

Natural adaptation is the policy equivalent of doing nothing. The "do nothing" approach does not imply that nothing is happening – it just means that there is no specific government policy aimed at responding to the climate change problem. A variation of the "do nothing" scenario is one in which the main policy reaction is to undertake further research. Characterizing such a scenario as "do nothing" may seem misleading, especially since "do nothing" might be taken to imply some reprehensible complacency on the part of governments. In fact, however, "doing nothing", or undertaking a "research-oriented-do-nothing" policy may be justified if it can be shown that (a) action now would be very expensive, or (b) more cost-efficient action might result from delaying the intervention policy.

Natural adaptation will not be costless. In an ideal world, we would be just as interested in the cost of this type of adjustment as we are in, say, the costs of building sea-wall defences as a deliberate measure to alleviate sea-level rise impacts. In practice, however, it is very unlikely that the costs of most of this gradual adaptation can be estimated.

Nevertheless, what we assume about society's gradual adaptation to climate change affects what we can assume about the nature, extent and importance of the socio-economic impacts of that change.

Policy response

Assuming that governments decide to respond to the reality of climate change, there is some uncertainty about how they will respond. Essentially, there are two basic types of response that are possible. One is to attempt to prevent the impacts *ex ante* (i.e., the anticipatory prevention approach). The other is to attempt to adapt *ex post* to the changes in climate in the most efficient manner possible (adaptation approach).

Under the anticipatory prevention scenario, various actions would be taken to reduce CO_2 and CFC emissions in an effort to contain future climate warming within an "acceptable" level. If, for example, the fuel mix is changed compared to what it would have been in the absence of climate change, we may presume that the change has positive costs (otherwise it would have been chosen anyway).

Under the adaptation scenario, various policy options exist. Adaptations may be as obvious as building higher sea-wall defences, or as broad as making changes in land-use planning practices. Expenditure on this type of policy will ameliorate the impacts of climate change after the changes have occurred.

The uncertainties about climate change are both scientific and socio-behavioral. We do not know enough at the moment to say what the average global temperature and sea-level rise will be. We know even less about the spatial distribution of the temperature rise, and hence an analysis of the regional impacts is necessarily speculative. Moreover, impacts depend on how people respond to climate warming and sea-level rise and on the kinds of actions that governments will take. All this suggests, strongly, that there has to be both a great deal more scientific research *and* socioeconomic research on climate change.

But now consider the policy implications of this uncertainty. Does it, for example, mean that we should *delay* action until the scientific and socioeconomic research narrows the range of uncertainty? On the contrary, there are at least four reasons for acting *now*. First, the outcome if the *worst* happens is clearly catastrophic. Unless we are positively in favour of bearing

Box 1.4   Climate change scenarios

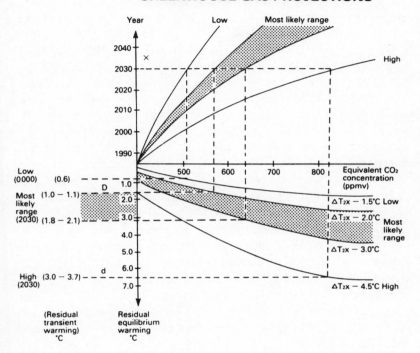

Source: R. Warrick, P. Jones, T. Russell, *The Greenhouse Effect, Climatic Change and Sea Level: an Overview*, Climatic Research Unit, School of Environmental Sciences, University of East Anglia, 1988.

risks, we need to undertake risk-averse policies. (This was the message of Box 1.2.) Second, the longer the world community delays action on the greenhouse effect the greater will be the "committed" level of warming (see Box 1.4). Delay is therefore not costless: the damage from greenhouse gases will simply be the greater the longer we delay. Third, the design of efficiently targeted policies should certainly wait for further information – it would be economic folly to engage in costly policies now if we can target them more efficiently later on. But a rational approach is to begin with the *low-cost* policies to contain greenhouse effects – *energy conservation* is the conspicuous example. Fourth, prevention must be international. But there are time lags in getting international cooperation. Indeed, the speed with which the Montreal Protocol on CFCs was obtained may be the exception, not the rule. For the costs to CFCs are insignificant compared to what must happen if the greenhouse effect is to be truly contained. There are reasons for believing that, even though the global benefits are large, the existence of substantial control costs could make global cooperation very difficult:[5] countries may not know if they will be gainers or losers, that some countries will partly gain and partly lose, and that we cannot yet say *when* these gains and losses will occur, and the difficulties of getting international agreement build up even further.

International cooperation to contain greenhouse effects to an "acceptable level" is vital and urgent. The urgency arises because of the nature of the risks if the worst outcome occurs; because the longer the delay the more the world is "committed" to increased warming and hence increased damage; because future adjustment is likely to be expensive; and because the only form of containment is through international cooperation which will be complex and difficult to secure. Global pollution problems underline the need for anticipatory policy.

Summarizing the sustainable development approach to environmental policy

The preceding discussion suggests that six factors – cost escalation, time preference, the informational value of delay, uncertainty, irreversibility and the underlying tenets of sustainable development – impacts on the nature of environmental policy as shown in Box 1.5.

Box 1.5 **Factors affecting the choice of environmental policy stance**

	Features favouring:	
	(a) Reactive policy	*(b) Anticipatory policy*
Time preference (discounting)	YES	NO
Information by delay	YES	NO
Cost escalation	NO	YES
Uncertainty	NO	YES
Irreversibility	NO	YES
Sustainable development	NO	YES

Overall, the result suggests strongly that a society committed to sustainable development will shift the focus of its environmental policy towards an anticipatory stance, especially as reactive policy risks shifting the burden of environmental risks to future generations. As the rest of this report will show, this has implications for the way in which the sustainable development ideal is translated into practical policy measures.

Growth versus the environment?

In the 1970s it was familiar for the debate about environmental policy to be couched in terms of economic growth versus the environment. The basic idea was that one could have economic growth – measured by rising real per capita incomes – *or* one could have improved environmental quality. Any mix of the two involved a *trade-off* – more environmental quality meant less economic growth, and vice versa. Perhaps the most forceful, if least scientific, expression of that view came with the publication of the Club of Rome's *Limits to Growth* in 1972.[6]

Box 1.6   **Characterization of two approaches to growth and the environment**

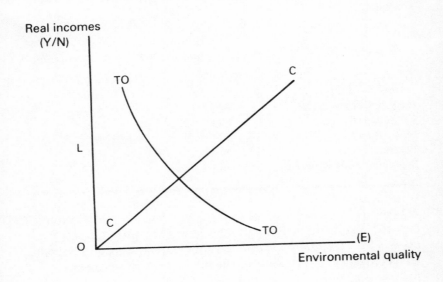

In this simplified diagram, society has to choose where to locate itself in terms of the amount of economic growth (an increase in real income per capita, Y/N) and the amount of environmental quality (E) that it wants. If growth can only ever be achieved at the expense of environmental quality, then society has to choose a point on TO-TO. If, on the other hand, growth and environment are wholly compatible, it chooses a point on C-C. A "limit to growth" could be typified by a point such as L where, hypothetically, growth brings about zero environmental quality – i.e. a "doomsday" solution.

The modern sustainable development debate has tended to shift the focus away from growth *versus* the environment to one of the potential *complementarity* of growth and environment. Box 1.6 shows how these two very contrasting approaches might be illustrated. The diagram measures economic growth on the vertical axis and environmental quality on the horizontal axis. If the "trade-off" view is correct then society has always to choose some point on a curve such as TO-TO: more growth means less environmental quality. If the "complementarity" view is correct then society is on some point on the curve C-C: more growth is quite compatible with more environmental quality.

In reality both approaches are unlikely to be correct.

The environmental "doomsters" have probably oversold the negative relationship between economic growth and environmental quality, and the advocates of "environmental quality through wealth creation" have similarly understated the potential for economic change to damage the environment.

It is doubtful if modern advocates of sustainable development belong in either of the two categories. There are various reasons for this:

(i) Sustainable development tells us that environmental quality frequently improves economic growth. It can do this by:

• improving the health of the workforce;
• creating jobs in the "environmental sector" (recreation, tourism);
• creating jobs in the "pollution abatement sector" (air and water pollution control equipment, clean-up campaigns).

(ii) Sustainable development shifts the focus from economic growth as narrowly construed in traditional attitudes to economic policy. It speaks of *development* rather than growth, of the quality of life rather than real incomes alone. That is, sustainable development makes it clear that the very antithesis of growth and the environment is not the issue.

(iii) Sustainable development accepts that there must be some "trade-offs" between narrowly construed economic growth and environmental quality. In that context it draws attention to two fundamental issues:

• If there is to be a trade-off, society must choose on the basis of a full understanding of the choice in question. That means the economic value of the environmental cost, if one is to be incurred, must be understood.

Rational trade-offs mean valuing the environment properly, an issue we have already seen that is at the heart of the sustainable development approach. There must be informed choice, not choice based on the presumption that the environment is a free good.

• Growth frequently conflicts with environment because all too often little effort is made to see how the environment might be integrated into capital investments and other decisions at the outset. Examples are numerous: we can have propellants in spray cans that do not harm the ozone layer, gasoline does not have to be leaded, energy can be conserved rather than used wastefully, and so on.

In short the issue is often not whether we grow or not, but *how* we grow. Modern technology offers many examples of how to save resources and energy – modern information and information transmission technology alone have the potential for saving on fuels and pollution. Technology is not, however, a "free gift" – it too comes with its own array of environmental problems.

(iv) Sustainable development accepts what many economists have been arguing for a long time, namely that what we have been calling "economic growth" in the past has been measured by some very misleading indicators. As Chapter 4 discusses in detail, the tendency has been to use a measure of gross (or sometimes net) national product (GNP or NNP) as the basis for economic growth calculations. If GNP increases that is economic growth. But GNP is constructed in a way that tends to divorce it from one of its underlying purposes: to indicate, broadly at least, the standard of living of the population. If pollution damages health, and health care expenditures rise, that is an increase in GNP – a rise in the "standard of living" – not a decrease. If we use up natural resources then that is capital depreciation, just as if we have machines we count their depreciation as a cost to the nation. Yet depreciation on man-made capital is a cost while depreciation of environmental capital is not recorded at all.

It is not really credible any longer to use the national accounts (the accounts that measure GNP and its constituents) to indicate the quality of life, although that does not mean that the accounts should be disbanded.

The "growth versus environment" debate is clearly still a real one in the sustainable development context. There will be situations in which growth involves the sacrifice of environmental quality, and where the conservation of the environment means forgoing economic growth. But sustainable development attempts to shift the focus to the opportunities for income and employment opportunities from conservation, and to ensuring that any trade-off decision reflects the full value of the environment.

In the latter respect the past failure to reflect environmental values fully in economic decision-making means that the trade-off decisions have been biased in favour of "growth" and against "environment". There can be no question that sustainable development makes the pendulum swing back towards the environment and public opinion in Europe also favours this swing (see Box 1.8).

There will be two opposite reactions to the idea that sustainable development calls for a *change of emphasis* in favour of the environment:

(1) Some conservationists will say that shifts of emphasis are not enough. There must be more radical change.

(2) Some industrialists and other "wealth creators" will say that the shift of emphasis will harm competitive power and

Box 1.7   The cost of past environmental policy in OECD countries

IMPACT ON GDP OR GNP (Difference in percentage points between level with and without environmental programmes)

Level of programme effort	Assumptions	In first year	After several years	In final programme year	After programme completion
AUSTRIA (1979-85)		*1979*		*1985*	
Base programme	No spare productive capacity	..		−0.2	
Base programme	Spare productive capacity	..		−0.2	
Increased programme	No spare productive capacity	..		−0.6	
Increased programme	Spare productive capacity	..		0.5	
FINLAND (1966–82)		*1976*	*1979*	*1982*	
Water pollution control		0.3	0.5	0.6	
FRANCE (1976–82)		*1966*	*1970*	*1974*	
Actual programmes implemented		–	–	0.1	
Increase in actual programmes		–	–	0.4	
NETHERLANDS (1979-85)		*1979*	*1982*	*1985*	*1987*
Base programme	No foreign inflation due to environment programme	0.1	−0.2	−0.6	−0.7
Base programme	Low foreign inflation due to environment programme	0.1	−0.2	−0.5	−0.7
Base programme	Medium foreign inflation due to environment prog.	0.1	−0.2	−0.5	−0.7
Base programme	High foreign inflation due to environment programme	0.1	−0.2	−0.5	−0.7
Base programme	Medium foreign inflation and no wage indexation	0.1	−0.1	−0.3	−0.4
NORWAY (1974-83)		*1974*	*1977*	*1983*	
Base programme	Partial shift of programme costs to prices	..	..	..	
Base programme	Total shift of programme costs to prices	..	..	1.5	
UNITED STATES (1970-87)		*1970*	*1982*	*1987*	
Actual and planned programmes		0.2	−0.3	−0.7	
Increase in planned programmes, 1979-81		..	−0.2	−0.6	
Reduction in programme, 1981-87		..	−0.4	−0.7	
Actual and planned programmes	Restrictive anti-inflationary monetary policy	0.2	−0.6	−1.1	

Past environmental programmes in OECD countries have probably reduced GNP a little below what it would otherwise have been. But several observations are in order. (i) The effects have been small. (ii) The effects are measured in terms of the *conventional* approach to measuring GNP, for example excluding the fact that environmental benefits should themselves be treated as "income". (iii) The effects on *employment* tend to be positive because of the increase in jobs associated with the pollution control industry. *Future* environmental policy could be significantly more expensive if major efforts are made to meet people's wishes for a better environment, in the face of difficult, large-scale problems such as global warming. That underlines the need to find the most cost-effective way of dealing with the new environmental challenge.

Source: OECD, "The Impact of Environmental Measures on the Rate of Economic Growth, the Rate of Inflation, Productivity and International Trade", OECD International Conference on *Environment and Economics*, Background Papers, Vol.1, 1984, p.140.

Box 1.8 **Public perceptions in the European Community of "growth versus the environment"**

	Development of the economy should take priority	A choice must be made between the two	Protecting the environment is essential	Don't know	Total
COMMUNITY	9	32	50	9	100
Belgium	8	49	35	8	100
Denmark	3	30	55	12	100
Germany	3	41	50	6	100
France	11	29	56	4	100
Ireland	23	26	40	11	100
Italy	6	32	55	7	100
Luxembourg	6	28	65	1	100
Netherlands	9	40	45	6	100
United Kingdom	11	32	48	9	100
Greece	12	23	47	18	100
Spain	12	17	47	24	100
Portugal	11	33	38	18	100

Whatever the *technical* features of the growth versus environmental choice, 50 per cent of Europeans say that environmental protection is essential. Only 9 per cent put "development" as a priority.

Source: European Commission, *The Europeans and their Environment in 1986*, Brussels.

hence the opportunity to create future wealth with which to compensate future generations.

The concerns of both groups might be met by seeing what practical changes could be made to the nature of economic management in the light of sustainable development. This is what the rest of this report considers. For the moment we might inspect Box 1.7 which shows some statistics of what *past* environmental policy has cost the industrialized nations of the world. It is not a significant sum. Nor is it easy to find examples of environmental policy having a significant impact on the competitive position of a nation pursuing a rigorous environmental policy. But if past environmental policy has cost comparatively little, is that much comfort if future environmental problems are going to be larger and hence more costly to combat? If that is true then it provides a compelling case for re-appraising the way in which we combat environmental degradation.

Notes

1. This is the "discounting" phenomenon. See Chapter 6.
2. An argument that is sometimes advanced. The idea is that as the resource becomes impaired it effectively becomes scarcer. Once the scarcity is perceived there may be forces which will cause a market to be generated. Thus what was once common land in England became "privatized" through enclosure. The doubts about this "evolutionary" approach to environmental problems are many. The main ones are (a) that it is not clear how many zero-priced resources could be made subject to exclusive ownership (the ozone layer, for example), and (b) that we have no guarantee that the evolution of such rights would take place in time to conserve those resources and prevent their extinction.
3. To economists this simple idea is embraced by the more sophisticated one of "Pareto optimality". Pareto optimality is achieved when it is not possible to make one person better off (improve his or her "welfare") without making another person worse off. Translated into the intertemporal sphere this means that Pareto optimality across time involves not conferring gains for one generation at the expense of another. The present, for example, must not be made better off at

the expense of the future. Pareto optimality is of course consistent with making the future better off so long as the present is not made worse off. This last proposition should serve to remind us that the future has an obligation to the present just as much as the other way round.

4. The United Kingdom Prime Minister acknowledged this possibility in her speech to the Royal Society, 27 September 1988: "For generations, we have assumed that the efforts of mankind would leave the fundamental equilibrium of the world's systems and atmosphere stable. But it is possible that with all these enormous changes (population, agricultural, use of fossil fuels) concentrated into such a short period of time, we have unwittingly begun a massive experiment with the system of this planet itself."

5. See, for example, Scott Barrett, "On the nature and significance of international environmental agreements", London Environmental Economics Centre.

6. See D. H. Meadows, D. L. Meadows, J. Randers and W. Behrens, *The Limits to Growth*, Earth Island, London, 1972. For a modern appraisal, which is generally favourable to the "limits" idea, see H. Daly, "The economic growth debate: What some economists have learned but many have not", *Journal of Environmental Economics and Management*, Vol.14, no.4, December 1987, pp.323–36.

2. THE MEANING OF SUSTAINABLE DEVELOPMENT

Chapter 1 indicated that sustainable development has, as its principal aim, the search for a path of economic progress which does not impair the welfare of future generations. It also suggested that the role of maintaining environmental quality in this process of sustainable economic progress must be ranked higher than in the past. Environment is important because:

- it contributes *directly* to the quality of life: people appreciate and value, in increasing terms, wildlife and countryside, peace and quiet and tranquillity, and the finer cultural inheritances of the past.
- it contributes *indirectly* to the quality of life: poor environments mean poor health, more stress and more social unrest.
- it contributes *directly* to economic growth, more narrowly defined as traditionally-measured rising real income per head, by creating business opportunities in leisure and tourism, and pollution abatement. This direct contribution may be offset by the cost burdens of environmental controls, but Chapter 1 suggested that, to date, environmental policy has been inexpensive. If it is likely to become more expensive, then it is doubly important to find the most efficient ways of maintaining environmental quality (see Chapter 7).
- it contributes *directly* to a more soundly based measure of economic growth, i.e. one in which unmarketed goods and services are treated "on a par" with marketed ones. Only the latter enter the current accounting conventions for measuring economic growth. Moreover, expenditures to *offset* environmental damage perversely appear to be a gain in national output as currently measured.

This chapter elaborates on the meaning of sustainable development. We begin by asking what is "development"?

Economic development, development, and economic growth

Development implies change leading to *improvement* or *progress*. Consequently, what constitutes "real" development is a normative or "value-laden" issue. *Economic development* is similarly value-laden. Not surprisingly, therefore, what constitutes economic development is also disputed. It clearly involves change or transformation. An economy which raises its per capita level of real income over time but does so without making any transformations in its social and economic structure is unlikely to be said to be "developing".

Economic development has something to do with achieving a set of social goals, goals which may change over time and which therefore make "economic development" a moving target to some extent.

It seems fair to say that a society experiencing economic development is likely to be experiencing a combination of three sets of changes:

(i) an advance in the "utility" which the individuals in society experience. Utility here simply means "satisfaction" or "wellbeing". A major contributing factor to advances in wellbeing is real income per capita. Such a statement would be (nearly unanimously) undisputed in a poor country. Some would dispute it for rich countries like the United Kingdom. Another factor contributing to utility or wellbeing is the general "quality of the environment" (see above). The wellbeing of the most disadvantaged in society must also be given greater "weight" in a developing society: if average wellbeing advances at the cost of a worsening of the position of the most disadvantaged it seems reasonable to say that such a society is *not* developing.

(ii) preservation of existing freedoms and advances in freedoms where existing ones are inadequate. The freedoms in question relate to freedom from ignorance, from poverty and from squalor.[1] Put positively, economic development involves advances in skills, knowledge, capability and choice.

(iii) self-esteem and self-respect. These concepts mean that a developing society is one in which a sense of independence is growing. It may be independence from domination by others or independence from the state.

Construed in this way, economic development is much wider in concept than *economic growth*. Economic growth is fairly uncontroversially defined as an increase over time in the level of real GNP per capita (or, sometimes, the real level of *consumption* per capita).[2]

This is important. For it means that prefixing "sustainable" to the term "development" separates *sustainable economic development* from *sustainable economic growth*. They are not the same.

None the less, sustainable development and sustainable growth are interlinked. A society which does not maintain or improve its real income per capita is unlikely to be "developing". But if it achieves growth at the expense of the other components of development it cannot be said to be developing either.

Achieving economic development without sacrificing an acceptable rate of economic growth may be said to define the problem of sustainable development.

Environment, development and growth

We have already seen that improving environmental quality can contribute both to development and to growth. But the costs of improving the environment may also detract from economic growth as traditionally measured.

It is important, then, to ensure that economic growth is measured "properly" and to establish the point that, on the basis of historical experience, environmental protection has been comparatively "cheap" in terms of forgone economic growth. It has *not* been an issue of making major sacrifices in economic growth in order to improve the environment.

We address the issue later on as to whether *future* environmental quality can be secured without bigger sacrifices of economic growth. For the moment we observe that growth does not *necessarily* involve environmental degradation. The view that it does is based on perfectly respectable intellectual foundations. If we look at the way in which environmental resources function in their interaction with the economy, it is clear that materials get used up in all economic processes. If the materials are in finite supply then, by definition, the faster is growth the faster is their depletion. That raises the prospect of "running out" of resources. Many materials can be recycled – i.e. reinjected into the economic system, thus reducing the demands placed on new, "virgin" materials. But there are limits to recycling: as products get used so many of the uses are "dissipative". Lead in petrol is a good example. We can recycle the lead from car batteries but not from petrol exhausts. These "limits to recycling" suggest other policies, for example not putting the lead into petrol in the first place. We might generally term this "product design for environmental benefit" and it is clear that there is a vast potential in such a simple idea.

Unlike materials, we cannot recycle energy at all. Once used it is dissipated. It has zero potential for recycling. But it has all the potential for "product redesign", for example by designing low-energy products and, very simply, by reducing energy waste.

In all likelihood it is not the running out of material and energy resources that will matter for foreseeable futures. It is another type of resource that is in scarce supply – the resource of the natural environment as repository for all the waste products associated with materials and energy use. It is the "waste sink" characteristics of environments that perhaps occasion the greatest concern. These are natural resources to be cared for just like energy and materials. They comprise the oceans, the atmosphere and troposphere, the rivers and lakes of the world and the land-based waste sites. Recycling, product redesign, conservation and low-waste technology can interrupt the flow of wastes to these resources, and that is perhaps the major feature of a sustainable development path of economic progress.

The essential point however is that the relationship between materials, energy flows and environmental waste sink capacity to economic growth is not immutable. It can be modified. If these ratios can be systematically reduced, then growth *with* environmental quality is feasible. Put another way, in so far as environmental quality is a vital feature of economic development, growth and development can be compatible. Making them so is the challenge of sustainable development. It is the *pattern* of growth that needs more attention in an effort to make it compatible with the traditional desirability of economic growth.

None of the "recipes" for achieving changes in the pattern of growth is novel. Product redesign, recycling, energy and materials conservation are all familiar. But their familiarity makes them no less relevant. Subsequent chapters will show how some changes in the way we manage the economy can contribute, substantially in our belief, to their achievement.

Sustainable development

As we saw, "development" is a value word. To some extent, many of the elements are captured by the economist's concept of *utility*, or, more familiarly, "wellbeing". Indeed, this is how most economists would probably interpret sustainable development, i.e. as sustainable utility. Put another way, the wellbeing of a defined population should be at least constant over time and, preferably, increasing for there to be sustainable development.[3] The wider concept of sustainable development is clearly more "fuzzy" and there are obvious problems in determining how to assess whether development has been sustained if some of the indicators increase and some decrease. But this latter problem is essentially one of political judgement, of determining what society thinks matters. As Box 0.1 showed, a modern-day "political weighting" for environmental quality would surely be significantly higher than it was, say, 20 or 30 years ago.

Box 2.1 highlights the essential distinctions between the concepts of sustainable economic growth and sustainable economic development.

Box 2.1   **Sustainable growth and sustainable development**

Economic growth means real GNP per capita is increasing over time. But observation of such a trend does *not* mean that growth is "sustainable".

Sustainable economic growth means that real GNP per capita is increasing over time *and* the increase is not threatened by "feedback" from either biophysical impacts (pollution, resource problems) or from social impacts (social disruption).

Sustainable development means that per capita utility or wellbeing is increasing over time.
or
Sustainable development means that a set of "development indicators" is increasing over time.

For *both* definitions of sustainable development, the same "feedback" requirements apply. The wider concept of sustainable development – the last one – allows for this by including environmental "requirements" a condition to be fulfilled before development can be said to be sustainable. The same analysis could be applied to the problem of "social feedback".

Sustainable development and the environment

One extremely important way of incorporating emphasis on the environment into sustainable development is to ensure that people's preferences for environmental quality are properly accounted for.[4]

Once again this is the issue of *valuation* referred to in Chapter 1. Put simply: If development is to be sustainable it must encompass a full appreciation of the value of the natural and built environment in terms of the direct and indirect contributions that environments make to people's wellbeing.

While the point may now seem obvious, it has considerable implications for the way in which a nation monitors its "development". It means that the focus of policy attention must be as much on, say, trends in river quality or ozone depletion as it is on rates of economic growth. Of course, all governments pay some attention to environmental quality. The message of sustainable development is that much *more* attention needs to be paid to environmental variables.

It should be as easy to see, at a glance, how the nation is faring environmentally as it is to see how it is faring "economically". Chapter 4 addresses this point in detail.

But is it enough to say that "environment matters" and that we should all take note of the fact? Some sort of guideline is needed as to how environmental considerations might be embraced.

One such guideline, embraced by the Brundtland Commission and by others (see Annex on p.173) is that we should leave the next generation a stock of "quality of life" assets no less than those we have inherited.

There are two interpretations of this idea:

(i) that the next generation should inherit a stock of wealth, comprising man-made assets and environmental assets, no less than the stock inherited by the previous generation;
(ii) that the next generation should inherit a stock of environmental assets no less than the stock inherited by the previous generation.

The difference between the two is simple. The first stresses all capital assets, man-made and "natural". The second emphasizes "natural capital" only.

Box 2.2 shows a schematic illustration of the way in which man-made and "natural" capital interact to contribute to human wellbeing.

Sustainable development as non-declining wealth

What is the justification for ensuring that the next generation has at least as much wealth – man-made and natural – as this one? The intuitive idea underlying this approach to sustainable development is that of *intergenerational equity*. What is being

Box 2.2   **Capital and the economic process**

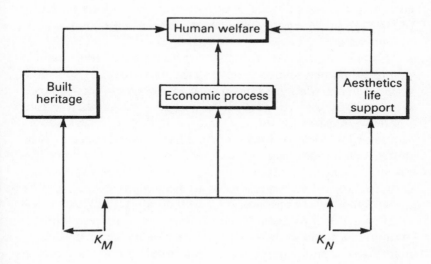

Man-made capital (K_M) contributes directly through capital investment to the economic process of production and hence consumption, which in turn directly affects human welfare. Natural capital (K_N) also contributes through, for example, the role that natural resources such as coal or oil play in manufacturing. K_M also contributes directly to human welfare through the construction of fine architecture. K_N contributes directly through the appreciation of natural landscapes, wildlife etc. The distinction between K_M and K_N is, of course, not precise. Man-made lakes or forests could be thought of as natural and man-made capital.

said is that we can meet our obligations to be fair to the next generation by leaving them an inheritance of wealth no less than we inherited.[5] Moreover, so long as each single generation does this, no single generation has to worry about generations far into the future. Each generation "looks after" the one that follows. On the face of it, this solves one otherwise intractable problem of deciding how far into the future one needs to look in order to decide how "sustainable" current development activity is.[6] In practice, problems remain because the effects of some current activities will spill over to many generations to come: the storage of some radioactive waste, for example, and the loss of biodiversity.

This suggests a variation on the "constant wealth" idea, namely that it should be pursued subject to the avoidance, as far as feasible, of *irreversibilities*. For once an irreversible effect occurs it is suffered by the next generation and all generations to come. There are reasons for thinking that most kinds of irreversibility will take the form of losses of "natural" capital: species loss, destruction of landscape or wetlands, coral reefs, primary forest and so on. Some natural capital can also be re-established: torn-up hedgerows can just as easily be replanted, trees can be grown, and, of course, many man-made alterations to natural environments have simply substituted one environment for another, sometimes with richer biodiversity than before. If man-made capital is destroyed it can usually be quickly rebuilt as our experience of reconstruction after wars or natural disasters shows. Built "heritage" cannot, of course, be reconstructed so that the loss of architectural heritage or ancient monuments or historically distinct settlements must also be classed as an irreversible loss.

This suggests that defining sustainable development as constant wealth inheritance is not sufficient. It requires modification to allow for the feasible avoidance of irreversible losses of natural assets, or compensation for their loss by other natural assets.

The "constant wealth" concept of sustainable development is open to the risk of political manipulation. Any government could always say that its particular form of economic management is designed to achieve wealth creation and that this will compensate the next generation for any losses it may have to bear. But the definition strictly should not permit such an interpretation because it unequivocally requires that the losses of natural assets be measured and valued on the same

basis as man-made capital. Thus, even on this broad definition of sustainable development the logical implication is that
economic development be measured so as to include changes in
environmental assets and quality, and that investment decisions
take environmental quality into account quite explicitly.

Sustainable development as non-declining natural wealth

The implicit assumption in the first definition of sustainable
development is that man-made and natural capital are *substitutes*. That is, so long as the overall *aggregate* of natural and
man-made capital does not decline between one generation
and the next, the stock of natural assets can decline because
the growth of man-made capital will compensate for it. This
picture is very much the "trade-off" picture shown in Box 1.6,
i.e. society as a whole can be better off through the depletion of
natural resources and environmental assets so long as it uses the
proceeds of that depletion to build up a stock of other assets.

The alternative approach is to focus on natural capital assets
and suggest that they should not decline through time. *Each
generation should inherit at least a similar natural environment*.
This interpretation seems consistent with many of the contributions made to the literature on sustainable development, and is
perhaps closest to that in some parts of the Brundtland Report.
In fairness, however, the broader "constant wealth" concept is
also consistent with the Brundtland Report in several places.

Why should the narrower focus be warranted? There are
several reasons:

(i) *Non-substitutability*. The essence of the "constant wealth"
argument is that we can switch between types of capital: they
are substitutes for each other. In reality this is true only up to
a point. There are many types of environmental asset for which
there are no substitutes. No one has yet found a way of (feasibly)
recreating the ozone layer, for example. The climate-regulating
functions of ocean phytoplankton, the watershed protection
functions of tropical forests, and the pollution-cleaning and
nutrient-trap functions of wetlands are all services provided by

natural assets and for which there are no ready substitutes. If man-made and natural capital are not so easily substituted, then we have a basic reason for protecting the natural assets we have.[7]

(ii) *Uncertainty*. Technological advances could of course advance the degree of substitution between the two types of capital. *Perhaps*, one day, we will not need the oceans for food or climate regulation, or the nutrient values of the world's coastal margins, but that raises the issue of how to behave if we cannot be certain that such substitution will take place. If we do not know an outcome it is hardly consistent with rational behaviour to act *as if* the outcome will be a good one. Most of society is "risk-averse": we act so as avoid bad consequences. If environmental risks have the potential for large negative payoffs (see Box 1.2) then risk-aversion dictates that we protect natural environments, at the very least until our understanding of how they function in terms of life-support grows.

(iii) *Irreversibility*. Irreversibility has already been discussed. It is an extreme form of non-substitutability. Once lost, no man-made capital can recreate a species, for example.

(iv) *Equity*. The poor are often more affected by bad environments than the rich. There is conflicting evidence as to how people value environments as their incomes change. Box 2.3 shows a suggested positive relationship between per capita gross domestic product (GDP) and "willingness to take action" about the environment. But willingness to take action is not the same as willingness to "pay" or "value" the environment. Researchers have found little evidence to support the idea that the rich are willing to *pay* more (relative to their income) than the poor for environmental quality.[8] But, if the linkage is unclear in the developed world, it is conspicuous in the developing world.

A constant or rising natural resource stock is most likely to serve the goal of intragenerational equity when the productivity of ecosystems is essential to the livelihoods of the poor. In such instances we are really talking about preserving *sustainable livelihoods*. This is most readily apparent in developing countries where rural livelihoods in particular are directly dependent on natural resources – i.e., dependent on woody biomass and

Box 2.3   **Average willingness to take action to protect the environment as a function of per capita GDP, by country**

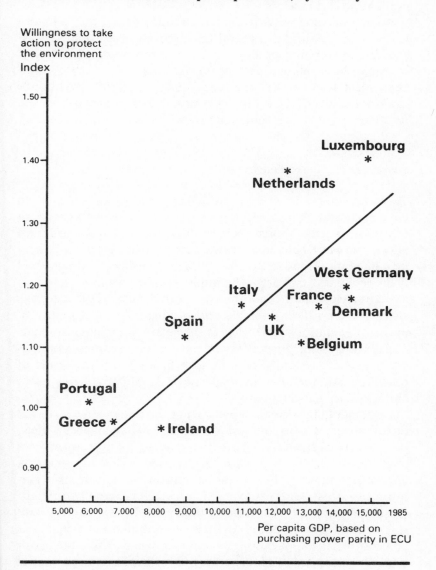

Willingness to take
action to protect
the environment
Index

vegetation for livestock fodder, fuelwood and raw materials; wildlife meat and fish for protein; crop residues, animal waste and organic matter for fertilizers; water supplies for domestic use; and so forth.

Where sustainability of the livelihoods of the poor is linked to the sustainability of natural resource use, the conflicts with equity are minimized. Conserving or improving the natural resource base allows an appropriate balance to be struck between the need for the poor to gain better livelihoods against the needs of future generations, or alternatively, the future needs of the present generation.

Sustainability as resilience

To understand the process by which ecosystems respond to environmental change, ecologists have developed the concept of *resilience* – the ability of the system to maintain its structure and patterns of behaviour in the face of external disturbance, i.e., its ability to adapt to change. This is usually distinguished from ecological *stability* – the ability of the system to maintain a relatively constant condition (its "equilibrium") in terms of its species composition, biomass and productivity, in response to normal fluctuations and cycles in the surrounding environment. The basic system properties for natural populations, communities and ecosystems are therefore *productivity* (in terms of numbers/biomass of individual species), *stability* (constancy) and *resilience* (sustainability).

Understanding ecological resilience in the face of external disturbances is also of importance to managed ecosystems, particularly agriculture where the purpose of human activity is to transform an ecosystem deliberately. The key question is whether or not the human modification and transformation of ecosystems affect their stability and resilience (sustainability). If the natural mechanisms of control and stabilization are replaced by increased human management and control, the application of human knowledge, and the use of both human and natural resources – all with minimum ecological disturbance – the result may be little change in ecological stability or sustainability.[9]

For both managed and natural ecosystems, the resilience of the system may differ depending on whether the external disturbance is a sudden shock or a cumulative, continuous stress. Especially for agricultural systems – or more appropriately "agro-ecosystems" – it may be more useful to define *sustainability* as the ability of an agro-ecosystem to maintain productivity when subject to stress or shock. *Productivity* can be re-defined as the output of valued product per unit of resource input, with common measures of productivity being yield or income per hectare, or total production of goods and services per household or nation. *Stress* in this context would be a regular, sometimes continuous, relatively small and predictable disturbance on agricultural productivity over time, for example the effect of salinity, toxicity, erosion, declining market demand or indebtedness. *Shock* on the other hand would be an irregular, infrequent, relatively large and unpredictable disturbance to the agricultural system, such as a rare drought or flood, a new pest or a sudden rise in input prices, like oil in the mid-1970s.

The unchecked abuse of resources within an *agro-ecosystem*, whether as a result of the inappropriate use of agro-chemicals and fertilizers, the overcropping of erodible soils, poor drainage, etc, not only directly affects the sustainability of the agro-ecosystem but may also increase its susceptibility to other external stresses and shocks, such as changes in market conditions, prolonged dry seasons, changes in land tenure, and so on.

As a consequence, a crucial component of sustainability, as defined in terms of the resilience of an agricultural system to external stresses and shocks, is maintaining the environmental resources and ecological functions upon which the system depends.

In the same way, we can consider the sustainability of an *economic* system in terms of its ability to maintain productivity when subject to stress on an economic system that may make it less "resilient" over time. In this context, "conservation of natural capital" essentially means exploiting the various functions of the environment – the production of material and energy inputs, the assimilation of waste and the maintenance of essential ecological functions and cycles – so as to minimize the stress imposed by environmental degradation on the economic system. Thus if the environment is likened to a stock of "natural" capital yielding a flow of services to the economic system (i.e., its essential economic functions), then sustainable development of that system involves maximizing the net benefits of economic development, subject to maintaining the services and quality of the stock of natural resources over time.

This rationale for natural capital conservation is often considered strongest for the developing world, where direct dependence on natural resource exploitation to sustain economic livelihoods, and in many cases to ensure economic growth and development, is so evident. But the rationale seems less applicable to advanced industrialized economies, with perhaps the exception of their agricultural and resource-based sector. The considerable accumulation and innovations in man-made capital and technology in these economies contribute to their resilience with respect to external acute or chronic shocks and stresses. Margins of flexibility are also greater than in poorer countries where population growth and poor economic performance in general often produce very narrow risk margins in the face of external disturbances, such as drought and changes in resource prices.

But the comparative resilience of advanced industrialized economies to environmental stresses and shocks might actually be illusory. First, although both man-made and natural capital contribute to the resilience of these economies, it does not imply that the two forms of capital are perfectly substitutible. As noted earlier, essential functions of the environment, such as complex life-support systems, biological diversity, aesthetic functions, micro-climatic conditions and so forth, have yet to be replicated by man-made capital, or can only be substituted at an unacceptably high cost. The risks of irreversible transformations of natural capital may therefore be high.

In addition, degradation of one or more parts of an ecosystem beyond some threshold level may lead to a breakdown in the integrity of the whole system, dramatically affecting recovery rates and resilience of the system. The total costs of the system breakdown may exceed the value of the activity causing the initial degradation.

Man-made capital often lacks an important feature of natural capital – *diversity*. The resilience justification for conserving the natural capital stock is thus based on the idea that diverse ecological and economic systems are more resilient to shocks and stress.

In turn, to maintain diversity it is essential to avoid irreversible choices. Since knowledge is rarely lost for ever, irreversibility involving man-made capital is rare – discontinued machines can be re-constructed, structures rebuilt, technology recreated, and so on. But ecological irreversibility is not unusual – natural species are lost every year, unique ecosystems are destroyed and environmental functions are irreparably damaged. This again reinforces the notion that we should only degrade or deplete our natural capital stock – particularly resources that may be irreversibly lost – if the benefits of doing so are very large.

In summary, then, conserving natural capital – ensuring that the natural environment is at least not degraded further – is consistent with:

● intergenerational equity
● intragenerational equity at least as far as poorer countries are concerned, and maybe also for richer countries
● resilience to stress and shock
● risk aversion

Various meanings of constant capital stock

Constancy of the natural capital stock can take on several different meanings. A common interpretation is in terms of constant *physical* capital stock. This is appealing for renewable resources, but, clearly, has little relevance to exhaustible resources since any positive rate of use reduces the stock. An alternative interpretation is in terms of a constant *economic value* of the stock. This allows for a declining physical stock with a rising real price over time, maintaining a constant economic value. The problem here is that the "price" variable needs to be interpreted with considerable care to reflect all the economic values deriving from multifunctional resources. Valuation problems, especially with functions such as contributions to reducing future catastrophes, are formidable. An additional complication lies with the presence of discontinuities in the valuation function, i.e. threshold effects such that stocks below a minimum critical level result in major costs.

A variant of the constant economic value concept is the view that a constant capital stock can be interpreted as one where the *price* of the stock remains constant over time. The motivation behind this idea is that scarcity can often be effectively measured in terms of the price of a natural resource, higher prices reflecting scarcity and lower prices reflecting abundance. This has some appeal in terms of exhaustible resources with uncertain reserves, where scarcity results in increased exploration effort or technological substitution. But for renewable resources current prices are less likely to reflect future scarcity. As an example, timber prices may remain constant in real terms despite stock reductions, because the *flow* of harvest is not significantly affected. Price may then rise only as the last units of the resource are extracted.

A broader version of the constant value rule would require that the total value of *all* capital stocks be held constant, manmade and natural. The basic idea here is that future generations would inherit a combined capital stock no smaller than the one in the previous generation. In this way a depleted resource, say oil, would be compensated for by other investments generating the same income. As already noted, if this view is accepted it is still clearly very important that natural capital stocks be correctly valued, and that threshold effects be allowed for.

In general, there is no easy interpretation to the idea of a constant capital stock. Some combination of an equal value rule with indicators of physical stocks to allow for critical minimum stocks (which, in turn, might qualify as "*sustainability indicators*") appears appropriate, but the issues have yet to be resolved. They should be the subject of further research.

Importing and exporting sustainability

It is perfectly possible for a single nation to secure a sustainable development path as defined in the main part of this chapter, *but at the cost of non-sustainability in another country*. This is perhaps most easily seen by considering an extreme example in which an economy imports all its raw materials, uses indigenous technology and human skills to convert it to a final product, and then exports the final product. Because it adds significant "value added" in the process it can then further import all its food needs as well. The nation's stock of natural resources remains intact, but the nations from which it imports may well be experiencing a decline in their natural capital stock because it is being exported.

To bring the extreme example closer to the real world, there are many countries which rely on imports of natural resources from developing countries which frequently do not have alternative products to sell in international markets. Consider the tropical hardwoods market. Five countries – Malaysia, Indonesia, Philippines, Ivory Coast and Gabon – supply some 80 per cent of the world market in tropical hardwoods. In roundwood equivalents, Japan accounts for about 50 per cent of these imports, and EEC for just under 40 per cent (see Box 2.4).

Yet it is clear that the tropical forests supplying these products are being used unsustainably. In so far as economic progress in the wealthier countries can be said to be sustainable (and this is something that needs testing with "sustainability indicators"), it could be said that the sustainability is in part being achieved by "importing" it through non-sustainability in other nations.

The situation may not be as bad as this. It depends first on how we define sustainability. If we take the broader view, based on total rather than natural capital only, the hardwood exporting countries may simply be converting their export revenues into investments which will sustain their future. In other words, they may be "swapping" natural for man-made capital. Unfortunately we have little evidence that this is happening, and a good deal of evidence that no such transformation is taking place. Instead, export proceeds are often turned into consumption, not into

Box 2.4   **Direct imports of tropical hardwood timber products: a comparison of imports in volume by Japan, the USA, Western Europe and the 12 EEC countries 1984** (in '000 cubic metres, real volumes and roundwood equivalents – RWE)

	Japan		USA		Western Europe		EEC	
	Real	RWE	Real	RWE	Real	RWE	Real	RWE
Logs	13,321	13,321	141	131	4,012	4,012	3,706	3,750
Sawnwood	628	1,143	424	772	2,837	5,163	2,760	5,019
Veneers	60	114	119	226	187	355	175	331
Plywood	64	147	1,095	2,519	974	2,239	888	2,047
Total RWE	–	14,725	–	3,658	–	11,769	–	11,147

Sources: UNECE/FAO, "Forest Products Markets in 1985 and Prospects for 1986", *Timber Bulletin*, Vol. XXXVIII no. 9.
UNECE/FAO, "Forest Products Trade Flow Data 1983–1984", *Timber Bulletin*, Vol. XXXVIII, no. 7.
FAO, Monthly Bulletin – "Tropical Forest Products in World Timber Trade", MISC/85/7, December 1985.

building up the capital base, investment. A further concern about the idea of "importing sustainability" is that the trade is "free", and free trade should be to the mutual advantage of all participating countries since it is based on the doctrine of comparative advantage.

This suggests that a nation which could be regarded as importing sustainability should seek to compensate the exporting nation for its loss. Essentially, the exporting nation risks non-sustainability for the benefit of the importing nation. In part its failure to manage its resources sustainably is a policy choice – it chooses to "mine" rather than "manage" its renewable resources. But we might legitimately argue that this is not the full story and that the importing nation has an obligation to reverse the flow of sustainability benefits. This idea takes us beyond the remit of the current report, but effectively it points us towards the importance of *foreign aid for sustainable development*.

Foreign aid for sustainable development recognizes that the wealthier countries of the world "import sustainability" from the poorer countries of the world. While non-sustainability in the exporting countries must be partly a matter of policy choice, there is a case for returning sustainability to the exporting nations through environmentally sensitive aid. Such aid would focus on securing sustainable resource management in the exporting nations.

Conclusions on the meaning of sustainable development

Economic development is broader in concept than economic growth. The latter relates to increases in a defined quantity, real GNP per capita. The former encompasses broader values as well such as the quality of life.

An economy experiencing economic growth over long periods cannot, however, be said to be on a *sustainable* growth path if there is evidence that the feedback from changes in environmental quality will induce non-sustainability.

Thus, even with a narrowly focused policy objective of economic growth the environment still "matters".

Sustainable development (as opposed to growth) involves at least all the things that impact on individuals' wellbeing (or "utility"), and, more loosely, factors such as freedoms and self-respect.

Sustaining development in these broader terms involves providing a bequest to the next generation of an amount and quality of wealth which is at least equal to that inherited by the current generation. It can be shown that such a "constant capital" bequest is consistent with the concept of intergenerational equity. Sustainable development is therefore partly about intergenerational equity.

On one view of sustainable development that bequest comprises a "mix" of man-made and "natural" capital. It is the aggregate quantity that matters and there is considerable scope for substituting man-made wealth for the natural environmental assets.

Even on this broad view of wealth bequest, sustainable development involves valuing the environment "properly". As long as the services of natural and other environments are treated as if they are "free goods" the wrong mix – from the standpoint of economic efficiency – of natural and man-made capital will emerge.

The broad concept of wealth bequest needs supplementing with a concern to avoid irreversible losses of environmental assets. But there are strong reasons to think of sustainable development as involving a further constraint, namely that the stock of environmental assets as a whole should not decrease. This is consistent with overall wealth increasing through time, but places greater emphasis on environmental conservation than the broad wealth bequest concept.

The rationales for conserving natural capital are several. It accounts for the lack of substitutability for many environmental functions, for uncertainty, and for resilience. It is consistent with some equity concerns, especially in the poorer parts of the world.

In the rest of this report we tend to adopt the "constant natural capital" approach to sustainable development and show how it might be made more operational. But it is important to understand that even if this approach is not accepted, and the broader wealth bequest approach is adopted, the general force of the conclusions to be derived still hold.

Notes

1. Here we have followed the classification of D. Goulet, *A New Concept on the Theory of Development* (New York: Atheneum Press, 1971).
2. GNP measures the output of all goods and services in the economy. Consumption relates only to those goods directly consumed by individuals. GNP would include the production of investment goods which yield a flow of consumption later on but not at the time of their investment.
3. Sustainable development as "non-declining utility" is elegantly investigated by John Pezzey in *Economic Analysis of Sustainable Growth and Sustainable Development*, Environment Department Working Paper No.15, World Bank, March 1989. A similar interpretation is to be found in Karl-Goran Maler, *Sustainable Development* (Washington DC: World Bank, Economic Development Institute, 1989). Both documents approach the subject from the standpoint of the theory of economic growth and are not easy reading. For the reasons given in the text, we prefer to keep the definition of sustainable development looser and to use it to embrace aspects of social development that are not captured by the notion of utility. Moreover, while, for example, Pezzey is critical of other approaches to sustainability because he feels they are non-operational, utility for a whole nation is non-measurable. The relevance of a non-measurable, non-comprehensive definition of sustainable development for policy purposes is thus very questionable. But this does not detract from the powerful insights into the concept of sustainable development that can be derived by adopting the "utility" approach.
4. Economists who advocate the "non-declining utility" definition of sustainable development do this by making environmental quality a factor in the "utility function". That is, utility, or wellbeing, depends on the consumption of goods and services *and* on environmental quality.
5. The intellectual foundations to this idea are clearly established in an elegant paper by Nobel Prize-winner Robert Solow, "On the Intergenerational Allocation of Natural Resources", *Scandinavian Journal of Economics*, Vol.88, no.1, 1986. Solow investigates

a theorem developed by another economist John Hartwick. Hartwick showed that a society with an exhaustible resource, such as oil, could enjoy a constant stream of consumption over time provided it invested all the "rents" from the exhaustible resource. (A "rent" is the difference between the price obtained for the resource and its costs of extraction.) What Solow shows is that the Hartwick rule is formally equivalent to *holding the overall capital stock constant.* The constant stream of consumption is then viewed as the interest secured on that "patrimony". The constant stream of consumption is, of course, one interpretation of intergenerational equity.

6. The *theoretical* approach in economics is to analyse the problem in terms of "infinite time horizons" – i.e. not to set any limit in time to the analysis. Again, this convention permits powerful techniques of analysis to be used. We do not adopt it here because the aim is to "translate", as far as possible, some of the findings of this economic analysis into politically more operational rules.

7. Note that the "constant wealth" argument does not *advocate* the destruction of natural wealth. It simply says that one should substitute for the other according to society's relative *valuations* of the two. Hence, once again, the importance of giving natural assets a "proper" valuation. Since many of them have no market price, allowing unfettered market forces to dictate the substitution is necessarily incompatible with sustainable development – see Chapter 7.

8. For a survey of the relationship between *willingness to pay* for environmental quality and income see David Pearce, "The social incidence of environmental costs and benefits", *Progress in Environmental Planning and Resource Management*, 2, 1980. Pearce found no evidence to support the notion of "environmental elitism" which he measured by the economist's concept of the "income elasticity of demand" – i.e. the percentage change in willingness to pay divided by the percentage change in income. There is a clear need to update and extend this survey, however.

9. Sustainable development as "resilience", particularly applied to agroecosystems, has been established by Gordon Conway in "The properties of agroecosystems", *Agricultural Systems*, Vol.24 (1987), pp. 95-117. See also Gordon Conway and Edward Barbier, *After the Green Revolution: Sustainable Agriculture for Development* (London: Earthscan Publications, forthcoming in 1990).

3. VALUING THE ENVIRONMENT

Chapters 1 and 2 showed that however sustainable development is interpreted it requires that we raise the political and economic profile of the environment. But there is an implicit bias in the way in which economies work. Many goods and services have prices which can be observed in the marketplace. Environmental goods and services and the general functions which environments serve (e.g. as a waste sink) are not invariably bought and sold in the marketplace. Thus if we leave the allocation of resources to the unfettered market, it will tend to *over-use* the services of natural environments.

This observation is elaborated upon in Chapter 7 and is a fundamental feature of economic science. In order to ensure a better allocation of resources, one that at least tries to correct the bias implicit in the unfettered marketplace, it is important to have some idea of what the environment is "worth". Chapter 1 stressed the importance of a proper *valuation* of the environment as a major feature of sustainable development. This notion offends some conservationists. It is therefore worthwhile explaining the basics of the economic valuation of environmental services.

Economics and environmental values

Care and concern for the environment can be thought of as positive preferences for cleaner air and water, less noise, protection of wildlife, and so on. Economics is about choice, and choice relates to situations in which we have preferences for certain things but in which we cannot choose everything we like because of income limitations. Very simply, given limited resources, the rational thing to do is to choose between our preferences in an effort to get the most satisfaction – or "welfare", to use the economist's term – we can. If we apply economics to environmental issues, then, we should expect to obtain some insights into the desirability of improving the environment further, taking the social objective of increasing people's overall satisfaction (or welfare) as given. This assumption about the social objective used to derive measures of gains and losses is important.

To be clear, what is being said is that an improvement in environmental quality is also an economic improvement if it increases social satisfaction or welfare.

Such a definition raises a host of questions and problems. For example, whose welfare are we talking about? It could readily be the case that we can improve this generation's welfare but only at the cost of the next generation's. Should we take this into account, and, if so, how? How far into the future should we look – a few generations, hundreds of years, or maybe thousands? Another problem concerns the legitimacy of measuring gains and losses according to how they impinge on human welfare alone. There is an extensive philosophical debate on the moral rights and standing of living creatures other than man: if they are ascribed rights, what relation do these rights have to human rights – are they equal, superior or less? A third problem (there are many more) is that a social objective based on mankind's more immediate wellbeing need not be consistent with long-run welfare or even human survival: while it is tempting to think that economic systems should contain some in-built mechanisms for sustainability, there is no evidence that they do. Some care needs to be exercised, then, that the use of social objectives such as gains in welfare does not dictate or support policies which are inconsistent with the ecological preconditions for existence or, at least, some minimal quality of life.

The preferences for the environment, which show up as gains in welfare to human beings, need to be measured. It may seem odd to speak of "measuring preferences" but this is exactly what that branch of environmental economics devoted to *benefit measurement* does. A benefit is any gain in welfare (or satisfaction or "utility"). A cost is any loss in welfare. We are concerned then with the measurement of the benefits from improvements in, or the costs of reductions in, environmental quality. If we prefer clean air, we place a value on it. But since clean air is not bought and sold in the marketplace, at least not directly, money is not directly involved. None the less, the benefit of clean air is an economic benefit – it improves the welfare of people.

In benefit estimation money is used as a measuring rod, a way of measuring preferences. There are very good reasons for supposing that money is a good measure of the gains and losses to people from environmental change. What is important is that money just happens to be a convenient measuring rod. As long as we do not forget that there will be some immeasurable gains and losses, the measurement of gains and losses in money terms will turn out to be revealing and, we shall argue, supportive of environmental values and environmental policy.

Although we limit money to being just a measuring rod, even this limited role for it still causes many people problems. For example, what does it mean to place a money value on the benefit of preserving the Californian condor or the African rhinoceros? The temptation is to say that such creatures are "beyond price".

There are, however, two interpretations that might be placed on the idea that something is priceless. The first is that priceless objects are of infinite money value. When art experts speak of priceless works of art, however, they do not mean that they have infinite values. They mean that they are unique and irreplaceable, but that, in auction they would fetch very high prices indeed. A moment's reflection will indicate that no one can or would pay an infinite price for them. So it is with the condor and the rhinoceros: their preservation is worth very large sums of money – many of us would pay substantial sums to see them preserved – but none of us values them at an infinite price. The equation of "priceless" with "infinite value" is illicit. The second interpretation is more appealing. This says that there are some things in life which simply cannot be valued in money terms – there is somehow a compartment of our thinking that refuses to place money values on, say, human life. While this is a more reasonable interpretation of phrases such as "beyond price" care needs to be taken in applying it. We do not act as if human life, for example, is outside our capacity to value things in money terms. We quite explicitly draw boundaries round the kinds of expenditures that we are prepared to make to save life. Thus, while there remains a quite warranted suspicion that the process of money valuation is illicit in some contexts, the reality is that choices have to be made in contexts of scarce resources. Money as a measuring rod is a satisfactory means of proceeding.

Environmental improvements can show up in the form of effects which have *direct money values*. Improving a beach or river or wetland area, for example, can increase the number of visitors and, if the area has entrance charges, the revenue from those charges will increase. Reducing air pollution can improve the growth and quality of agricultural crops and there is obviously a direct monetary counterpart to such gains. Reducing sulphur emissions may lower the rate at which buildings or metal structures corrode. The direct market value of such reduced corrosion can be estimated by looking at the prolonged life of the structures and hence the reduced cost of protecting them or replacing them. Slightly less obvious is the effect that improving human health has on the saving of marketed resources. Reductions in respiratory disease from reducing air pollution, for example, will show up in a reduced demand for health care, thus saving on health service costs, and in less days lost from work due to illness. Notice, however, that these gains in reduced resource costs and increased productivity are not adequate measures of the welfare gain. This can only be measured by the value placed on improved health by the person at risk, and, typically, this will bear little relation to the resource costs that are saved. We shall return to this issue later.

The above examples indicate some of the ways that we can approach the monetary evaluation of the welfare gains from environmental improvement. But many of the gains will not show up even in such an indirect fashion. Suppose for example that the improved wilderness area is not subject to entrance charges but that because of the improvements more people do visit it. There is no apparent "market" in the environmental improvement: the gain is not bought and sold by anyone.

It is important to realize that, while the absence of markets or indirect markets makes the process of economic evaluation more difficult, it by no means renders it impossible. Even more important, the absence of a market or indirect market does not mean that economic gains are not present. There are still welfare improvements – people prefer the wilderness area to be improved. This preference has to be measured.

The uses of monetary measures

Why is it important to place monetary measures on environmental gains and losses? There are several reasons.

Preferences for environmental improvement can show up in various ways. We have already noted, for example, that membership of environmental bodies responds to increased awareness. Political lobbies are another mechanism, not unrelated to membership of pro-environment organizations, and the concern of political parties to secure the "green vote" is another manifestation of the importance of environmentalism. Both expressions of concern capture to some extent the intensity of preference for the environment, but the attraction of placing money values on these preferences is that they measure the *degree* of concern. The way in which this is done is by using, as the means of "monetization", the willingness of individuals to pay for the environment.

At its simplest, what we seek is some expression of how much people are willing to pay to preserve or improve the environment. Such measures automatically express not just the fact of a preference for the environment, but also the intensity of that preference. Instead of "one man one vote", then, monetization quite explicitly reflects the depth of feeling contained in each vote.

If, of course, the issue is one of losing an environmental benefit, we may wish to rephrase the problem in terms of individuals' willingness to accept monetary compensation for the loss, rather than their willingness to pay to prevent the loss. This can result in very large implied values of environmental quality. Our first reason for seeking a monetary measure, then, is that it will, to some considerable extent, reflect the strength of feeling for the environmental asset in question.

The second reason arises out of the first: provided the monetary measures that are revealed are sufficiently large, they offer a supportive argument for environmental quality. The usefulness of such arguments in turn arises from the fact that voters, politicians and civil servants are readily used to the meaning of gains and losses that are expressed in pounds or dollars.

To say that a particular species in danger from some development is valued very highly because of the vocal expression of concern is one thing. To support that argument with a monetary expression of that concern makes the case for preservation stronger than if any one argument is used alone.

The third reason for wanting to make the effort at monetization is that it may permit comparison with other monetary benefits arising from alternative uses of funds.

The point here is that preserving and improving the environment is never a free option: it costs money and uses up real resources. This is true whether actual expenditures are incurred to preserve a habitat or insulate houses against noise or introduce sulphur emission reductions, or whether the cost of preservation is in terms of some benefit forgone. Preserving a wetlands area, for example, may well be at the cost of agricultural output had the land been drained. If a monetary measure of environmental benefits can be secured, it can be compared to the monetary benefits of the agricultural output. This will help in any analysis of the extent to which it is socially worthwhile to preserve the land. The option with the biggest net benefit – i.e. the excess of benefits over costs – will be the one that is preferred, subject to any other considerations relating, say, to the interests of future generations.

The reasoning above may be formalized. The exercise of comparing the costs and benefits of two or more options of the use of land in the manner discussed is known as cost–benefit analysis.

Cost-benefit analysis (or CBA for short) makes operational the very simple, and rational, idea that decisions should be based on some weighing up of the advantages and disadvantages of an action.

At the moment, it is important to stress that CBA is not the only way to assist in decisions of the kind under consideration. There are other approaches which may be preferred. But CBA is the only one which explicitly makes the effort to compare like with like using a single measuring rod of benefits and costs, money.

Monetary value of national environmental damage and benefits

It is possible to illustrate the way in which benefit estimation techniques have been used to measure the importance of damage to the environment and, the converse, the benefits of environmental policy.

Box 3.1 **Pollution damage in the Netherlands** (all figures are in billions)

	Cumulative Damage to 1985		Annual Damage 1986	
	Dfl	*US$*	*Dfl*	*US$*
Air pollution	4.0–11.4	1.2–3.0	1.7–2.8	0.5–0.8
Water pollution	n.a.	n.a.	0.3–0.9	0.1–0.3
Noise nuisance	1.7	0.5	0.1	0.0
Total	5.7–13.0	1.7–3.5	2.1–3.8	0.6–1.1

Source: Netherlands Ministry of Public Housing, Physical Planning and Environmental Management, *Environmental Program of the Netherlands 1986–1990* (The Hague, 1985); and J. B. Opschoor, "A Review of Monetary Estimates of Benefits of Environmental Improvements in the Netherlands", OECD Workshop on the Benefits of Environmental Policy and Decision-Making, Avignon, France, October 1986.

Box 3.1 shows estimates for the costs of environmental damage in the Netherlands. Note that these are damage estimates arising from pollution. A good many types of damage were not capable of "monetization", so that, if the monetized figures are accepted, actual damage exceeds the estimates shown. Various techniques were used to derive the figures and considerable caution should be exercised in using them. They are, at best, "ballpark" numbers. None the less, they show that even measured damage is a significant cost to the economy – the totals shown are 0.5–0.9 per cent of Netherlands GNP.

Box 3.2 present similar estimates for Germany. Again, many items have not been valued and differing techniques are used to derive the estimates. The figures shown total over 100 billion

---

Box 3.2   **Pollution damage in Germany**

	1983/5	
	DM billion	*US$ billion*
Air pollution		
Health (respiratory disease)	2.3–5.8	0.8–1.9
Materials damage	2.3	0.8
Agriculture	0.2	0.1
Forestry losses	2.3–2.9	0.8–1.0
Forestry recreation	2.9–5.4	1.0–1.8
Forestry – other	0.3–0.5	0.1–0.2
Disamenity	48.0	15.7
Water pollution		
Freshwater fishing	0.3	0.1
Groundwater damage	9.0	2.9
Recreation	n.a.	n.a.
Noise		
Workplace noise	3.4	1.1
House price depreciation	30.0	9.8
Other	2.0	0.7
Total	103.0	33.9

Source: adapted from data given in W. Schulz, "A Survey on the Status of Research Concerning the Evaluation of Benefits of Environmental Policy in the Federal Republic of Germany", OECD Workshop on the Benefits of Environmental Policy and Decision Making, Avignon, France, 1986.

Deutschmarks annual damage (about US$ 34 billion), the major part of which is accounted for by the disamenity effects of air pollution (which is likely to include some of the separately listed air pollution costs), and the effects of noise nuisance on house values. The important point is that, if the estimates can be accepted as being broadly in the area of the true costs, pollution damage was costing an amount equal to 6 per cent of Germany's GNP in 1985.

Box 3.3 shows estimates for the USA for the year 1978. However, in this case the figures are for *damage avoided* by environmental policy. That is, taking the total of $26.5 billion, the argument is that, in the absence of environmental policy,

---

Box 3.3 The benefits of pollution control in the USA 1978

	US$ billion
Air pollution	
Health	17.0
Soiling and cleaning	3.0
Vegetation	0.3
Materials	0.7
Property values[1]	0.7
Water pollution[2]	
Recreational fishing	1.0
Boating	0.8
Swimming	0.5
Waterfowl hunting	0.1
Non-user benefits	0.6
Commercial fishing	0.4
Diversionary uses	1.4
Total	26.5

Source: M. Freeman, *Air and Water Pollution Control: a Benefit-Cost Assessment* (New York: Wiley, 1982).
Notes: 1. Net of property value changes thought to be included in other items.
　　　　2. At one half the values estimated for 1985.

---

pollution damage would have been $26.5 billion higher in 1978 than it actually was. The total shown in Box 3.3 would be 1.25 per cent of GNP in 1978. The marked divergence between this figure and the percentage suggested for Germany is partly explained by the absence of estimates for noise nuisance, and by the very low figure for property value changes.

Total economic value

While the terminology is still not agreed, environmental economists have gone some considerable way towards a taxonomy of economic values as they relate to natural environments. Interestingly, this taxonomy embraces some of the concerns of the environmentalist. It begins by distinguishing user values from "intrinsic" values. User values, or user benefits, derive from the actual use of the environment. An angler, wildfowl hunter, fell walker, ornithologist, all use the natural environment and derive benefit from it. Those who like to view the countryside, directly or through other media such as photograph and film, also "use" the environment and secure benefit. The values so expressed are economic values in the sense we have defined. Slightly more complex are values expressed through *options* to use the environment, that is, the value of the environment as a potential benefit as opposed to actual present use value. Economists refer to this as *option value*. It is essentially an expression of preference, a willingness to pay, for the preservation of an environment against some probability that the individual will make use of it at a later date. Provided the uncertainty about future use relates to the availability, or "supply", of the environment, the theory tells us that this option value is *likely* to be positive. In this way we obtain the first part of an overall equation for total economic value (TEV). This equation says:

TOTAL USER VALUE = ACTUAL USE VALUE + OPTION VALUE

Intrinsic values present more problems. They suggest values which are in the real nature of the thing and unassociated with actual use, or even the option to use the thing. "Intrinsic" value is a value that resides "in" something *and that is unrelated to human beings altogether*. Put another way, if there were no humans, some people would argue that animals, habitats etc. would still have "intrinsic" value. There is a separate, but not wholly independent, concept of intrinsic value, namely value that resides "in" something but which is captured by people through their preferences in the form of non-use value. It is this second definition of intrinsic value that we use. That is, values are taken to be entities that reflect people's preferences, but those values *include* concern for, sympathy with and respect for the rights or welfare of non-human beings. The briefest introspection will confirm that there are such values. A great many people value the remaining stocks of blue, humpback and fin whales. Very few of those people value them in order to maintain the option of seeing them for themselves. What they value is the *existence* of whales, a value unrelated to use, although, to be sure, the vehicle by which they secure the knowledge for that value to exist may well be a film or photograph or the recounted story. The example of the whales can be repeated many thousands of times for other species, threatened or otherwise, and for whole ecosystems such as rainforests, wetlands, lakes, rivers, mountains and so on.

The *existence values* are certainly fuzzy values. It is not very clear how they are best defined. They are not related to vicarious benefit, i.e. securing pleasure because others derive a use value. Vicarious benefit belongs in the class of option values, in this case a willingness to pay to preserve the environment for the benefit of others. Nor are existence values what the literature calls *bequest values*, a willingness to pay to preserve the environment for the benefit of our children and grandchildren. That motive also belongs with option value. Note that if the bequest is for our immediate descendants we shall be fairly confident at guessing the nature of their preferences. If we extend the bequest motive to future generations in general, as many environmentalists would urge us to, we face the difficulty of not knowing their preferences. This kind of uncertainty is different to the uncertainty about availability of the environment in the future which made option value positive. Assuming it is legitimate to include the preferences of as yet unborn individuals, uncertainty about future preferences could make option value negative.

Provisionally, we state that:

INTRINSIC VALUE = EXISTENCE VALUE

Thus we can write our formula for total economic value as:

TOTAL ECONOMIC VALUE = ACTUAL USE VALUE + OPTION VALUE + EXISTENCE VALUE

Within this equation we might also state that:

OPTION VALUE = VALUE IN USE (by the individual) + VALUE IN USE BY FUTURE INDIVIDUALS (descendants and future generations) + VALUE IN USE BY OTHERS (vicarious value to the individual)

The context in which we tend to look for total economic values should also not be forgotten. As discussed in Chapter 2, in many of those contexts three important features are present. The first is *irreversibility*. If the asset in question is not preserved it is likely to be eliminated with little or no chance of regeneration. The second is *uncertainty*: the future is not known, and hence there are potential costs if the asset is eliminated and a future choice is forgone. A dominant form of such uncertainty is our ignorance about how ecosystems work: in sacrificing one asset we do not know what else we are likely to lose. The third feature is *uniqueness*. Some empirical attempts to measure existence values tend to relate to endangered species and unique scenic views. Economic theory tells us that this combination of attributes will dictate preferences which err on the cautious side of exploitation. That is, preservation will be relatively more favoured in comparison to development.

Total economic value and decision-making

The relevant comparison when looking at a decision on a development project is between the cost of the project, the benefits of the project, and the TEV that is lost by the development. More formally, we can write the basic rules as:

(i) proceed with the development if

$$(B_D - C_D - B_P) > 0$$

and

(ii) do not develop if

$$(B_D - C_D - B_P) < 0$$

where

B_D refers to the benefits of development
C_D refers to the costs of the development, and
B_P refers to the benefits of preserving the environment by not developing the area.

TEV is in fact a measure of B_P, the total value of the asset left as a natural environment. The benefits and costs of the development will be relatively simple to measure, primarily because they are likely to be in the form of marketed inputs and outputs which have observable prices. This is clearly not going to be the case with TEV, so we need now to investigate ways in which we can measure the component parts of TEV.

Direct and indirect valuation

The approaches to the economic measurement of environmental benefits can be broadly classified as *direct* and *indirect* techniques. The former considers environmental gains – an improved scenic view, better levels of air quality or water quality, etc. – and seeks directly to measure the money value of those gains. This may be done by looking for a *surrogate market* or by using *experimental* techniques.

The surrogate market approach looks for a market in which goods or factors of production (especially labour services) are bought and sold, and observes that environmental benefits or costs are frequently attributes of those goods or factors. Thus, a fine view or the level of air quality is an attribute or feature of a house, a risky environment may be features of certain jobs, and so on. The experimental approach simulates a market by placing respondents in a position in which they can express their hypothetical valuations of real improvements in specific environments. In this second case, the aim is to make the hypothetical valuations as real as possible.

Indirect procedures for benefit estimation do not seek to measure direct revealed preferences for the environmental good in question. Instead, they calculate a "dose-response" relationship between pollution and some effect, and only then is some measure of preference for that effect applied. Examples of dose-response relationships include the effect of pollution on health; the effect of pollution on the physical depreciation of material assets such as metals and buildings; the effect of pollution on aquatic ecosystems, and the effect of pollution on vegetation.

However, indirect procedures do not constitute a method of finding willingness to pay (WTP) for the environmental benefit (or the willingness to accept (WTA) compensation for environmental damage suffered). What they do is to estimate the relationship between the "dose" (pollution) and the non-monetary effect (health impairment, for example). Only then do they apply WTP measures taken from direct valuation approaches. Accordingly, we do not discuss indirect procedures further in this chapter.

The hedonic price approach

The value of a piece of land is related to the stream of benefits to be derived from that land. Agricultural output and shelter are the most obvious of such benefits, but access to the workplace, to commercial amenities and to environmental facilities such as parks, and the environmental quality of the neighbourhood in which the land is located, are also important benefits which accrue to the person who has the right to use a particular piece of land. The property value approach to the measurement of benefit estimation is based on this simple underlying assumption. Given that different locations have varied environmental attributes, such variations will result in differences in property values. With the use of appropriate statistical techniques the hedonic approach attempts to (a) *identify* how much of a property differential is due to a particular environmental difference between properties and (b) *infer* how much people are willing to pay for an improvement in the environmental quality that they face and what the social value of the improvement is. Both the identification and the inference involve a number of issues which are discussed in some detail below.

The identification of a property price effect due to a difference in pollution levels is usually done by means of a *multiple regression* technique in which data are taken either on a small number of similar residential properties over a period of years (time series), or on a larger number of diverse properties at a point in time (cross section), or on both (pooled data). In practice almost all property value studies have used cross section data, as controlling for other influences over time is much more difficult.

It is well known of course that differences in residential property values can arise from many sources, such as the amount and quality of accommodation available, the accessibility of the central business district, the level and quality of local public facilities, the level of taxes that have to be paid on the property, and the environmental characteristics of the neighbourhood, as measured by the levels of air pollution, traffic and aircraft noise, and access to parks and water facilities. In order to pick up the effects of any of these variables on the value of a property, they *all* have to be included in the analysis. Hence such studies usually involve a number of *property* variables, a number of *neighbourhood* variables, a number of *accessibility* variables and finally the *environmental* variables of interest. If any variable that is relevant is *excluded* from the analysis then the estimated effects on property value of the included variables could be biased. Whether the bias is upward or downward will depend on how

Box 3.4   **Impact of air pollution on property values**

City	Year of: (a) property data (b) pollution measure	Pollution	% fall in property value per % increase in pollution
St Louis	1960	Sulphation	0.06–0.10
	1963	Particulates	0.12–0.14
Chicago	1964–7	Particulates	0.20–0.50
	1964–7	and Sulphation	
Washington	1970	Particulates	0.05–0.12
	1961–7	Oxidants	0.01–0.02
Toronto-	1961	Sulphation	0.06–0.12
Hamilton	1961–7		
Philadelphia	1960	Sulphation	0.10
	1969	Particulates	0.12
Pittsburg	1970	Dustfall and	0.09–0.15
	1969	Sulphation	
Los Angeles	1977–8	Particulates	
	1977–8	and Oxidants	0.22

Source: D. W. Pearce and A. Markandya, *Environmental Policy, Benefits: Monetary Evaluation* (Paris: OECD, 1989).

the included and excluded variables relate to each other and to the value of the property.

On the other hand if a variable that is irrelevant is included in the analysis then no such systematic bias results, although the estimates of the effects of the included variables are rendered somewhat less reliable. This would suggest then that we include as many variables as possible. However, doing so creates another difficulty. Typically many of the variables of interest are themselves very closely correlated. So, for example, accessibility to the town centre is often closely related to some measures of air pollution, and one measure of air pollution, such as total suspended particulate matter, is very closely correlated to other measures such as sulphur dioxide. To overcome this, many studies use only one "representative" measure of pollution.

Examples of hedonic price estimates of environmental quality

Box 3.4 reports the results of hedonic price air pollution studies where significant effects of air pollution on property values have been found and where these effects can be expressed irrespective of the units of measurement of pollution or property values (i.e. in percentage terms). As stated earlier, many such studies find it difficult to distinguish between different forms of air pollution because of their strong inter-correlation. In these

---

Box 3.5   **The impact of aircraft noise on house prices** (per cent of house price)

Location	Impact of one unit change in NEF	Impact of one unit change in NNI
USA		
Los Angeles	–	0.78
Englewood	–	0.78
New York	1.60–2.00	0.78
Minneapolis	0.40	0.62
San Francisco	0.50	0.45–0.90
Boston	0.40	–
Washington, DC	1.00	–
Dallas	0.58–0.80	–
Rochester	0.55–0.68	–
UK		
Heathrow (a)	0.56–0.68	–
(b)	–	1.12
Gatwick	–	1.46
Canada		
Toronto	–	0.18–0.60
Edmonton	0.50	–
Australia		
Sydney	0.00–0.40	–

Source: Pearce and Markandya, op. cit.

---

cases the one pollution measure included inevitably picks up the effects of all forms of air pollution with which it is strongly correlated. The results suggest that a one per cent increase in sulphation levels will result in falls in property values between 0.06 and 0.12 per cent. A similar increase in particulates lowers property values by between 0.05 and 0.14 per cent. Where the pollution variable is picking up more than one measure of air pollution, property value falls of between 0.09 and 0.5 per cent are recorded. Again we should note that the fall in property values per unit increase in pollution could vary with the level of pollution.

Boxes 3.5 and 3.6 show similar valuation approaches for noise nuisance. From Box 3.5 we would conclude that a unit increase in noise exposure frequency (NEF) will cause a 0.6 per cent reduction in the price of a house. (This is the average

---

Box 3.6   **The impact of traffic noise on house prices** (per cent of house price)

Location	Impact of one unit change in Leq
USA	
North Virginia	0.15
Tidewater	0.14
North Springfield	0.18–0.50
Towson	0.54
Washington DC	0.88
Kingsgate	0.48
North King County	0.30
Spokane	0.08
Chicago	0.85
Canada	
Toronto	1.05

Source: Pearce and Markandya, op. cit.

---

of the results reported in the NEF column.) Using a different measure of noise exposure, the noise and number index (NNI), the depreciation is just over 0.75 per cent for each unit of NNI. If these results applied today, what we would be saying is that aircraft noise causing a single unit change in the NNI measure of noise would "cause" a £3,750 reduction in the price of a house costing £50,000. From Box 3.6 we would conclude that an increase in traffic noise of one decibel will lower house prices by half of one per cent. Thus a house over £50,000 would lose £250 in value for every one-decibel increase in traffic noise.

Are hedonic price valuations reliable and accurate? The difficulty, of course, is that we have no absolutely correct yardstick against which to measure their reliability. If we had such a yardstick we would not need to engage in hedonic price approaches! It is thus in the *nature* of non-market valuation that accuracy and reliability have to be tested by other means. The main tests are:

(i) consistency of results in similar contexts;
(ii) consistency of results with *other* benefit estimation techniques;
(iii) consistency of results with "real market" experience.

On the basis of these tests, hedonic price valuation, properly executed, provides reasonably reliable benefit estimates.

Contingent valuation

The contingent valuation method (CVM) uses a direct approach – it basically asks people what they are willing to pay for a benefit, and/or what they are willing to receive by way of compensation to tolerate a cost. This process of "asking" may be either through a direct questionnaire/survey or by experimental techniques in which subjects respond to various stimuli in "laboratory" conditions. What is sought are the personal valuations of the respondent for increases or decreases in the quantity of some good, contingent upon an hypothetical market. Respondents say what they would be willing to pay or willing to accept *if* a market existed for the good in question. A contingent market is taken to include not just the good itself (an improved view, better water quality etc.), but also the institutional context in which it would be provided, and the way in which it would be financed.

One major attraction of CVM is that it should, technically, be applicable to all circumstances and thus has two important features:

● it will frequently be the *only* technique of benefit estimation;
● it should be applicable to most contexts of environmental policy.

The aim of the CVM is to elicit valuations – or "bids" – which are close to those that would be revealed if an actual market existed. The hypothetical market – the questioner, questionnaire and respondent – must therefore be as close as possible to a real market. The respondent must, for example, be familiar with the good in question. If the good is improved scenic visibility, this might be achieved by showing the respondent photographs of the view with and without particular levels of pollution. The respondent must also be familiar with the hypothetical means of payment – say a local tax or direct entry charge – known as the payment *vehicle*.

The questioner suggests the first bid (the "starting-point bid (price)") and the respondent agrees or denies that he/she would be willing to pay it. An iterative procedure follows: the starting-point price is increased to see if the respondent would still be willing to pay it, and so on until the respondent declares he/she is not willing to pay the extra increment in the bid. The last accepted bid, then, is the maximum willingness to pay (MWTP). The process works in reverse if the aim is to elicit *willingness to accept* (WTA): bids are systematically lowered until the respondent's minimum WTA is reached.

A very large part of the literature on CVM is taken up with discussion about the "accuracy" of CVM. Accuracy is not easy to define. But since the basic aim of CVM is to elicit "real" values, a bid will be accurate if it coincides (within reason) with one that would result if an actual market existed. But since actual markets do not exist *ex hypothesi* (otherwise there would be no reason to use the technique), accuracy must be tested by seeing that:

• the resulting bid is similar to that achieved by other techniques based on surrogate markets (house price approach, wage studies, etc.);
• the resulting bid is similar to one achieved by introducing the kinds of incentives that exist in real markets to reveal preference.

One significant feature of the CVM literature has been its use to elicit the different kinds of valuation that people place on environmental goods. In particular, CVM has suggested that existence values may be very important, as we shall see.

Travel-cost approaches

Travel-cost models are based on an extension of the theory of consumer demand in which special attention is paid to the value of time. That time is valuable is self-evident. What precisely its value is remains a question on which there is some disagreement, as will become clear later. However, as a starting point let us imagine a household consisting of a single person who works as a driver. He can work as many or as few hours as he wishes and he earns £5 an hour. He is fortunate enough not to pay taxes, and enjoys (or dislikes) driving for work or for recreation equally much. On a particular day he can either drive to a park that takes an hour to get to, and spend some time there, or he can go to work. In these circumstances he is faced with possibly two decisions. The first is whether to go to the park or to go to work. The second is, if he goes to the park, how much time to spend there. Suppose that the cost of the journey in terms of petrol and wear and tear is £3 and there is an entry fee of £1. If he goes to the park and spends a couple of hours there, then it will have cost him £4 in cash

Box 3.7   **Hypothetical relationship between recreational visits and visiting costs**

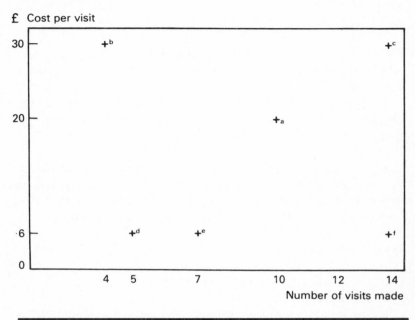

plus the loss of income £20. The true cost of the visit consists of the entry fee, plus the monetary costs of getting there, plus the forgone earnings. If we had information on all these variables, and we could obtain it for a large number of individuals, along with the information on the number of visits that each had made (and would make) during the season, then we could attempt to estimate the household's willingness to pay for a given number of visits. However, at first glance the data would not look very orderly. Box 3.7 shows the kind of data that we might find. Our single-earner household, for example, could be represented by the point **a**: he makes 10 visits at a cost per visit of £20. Points **b** and **c** represent two households, each of whom face a very high cost (£30). Of these **b** makes very few visits because it is a poor household living far from the recreational site, and **c** is a high-earning household located near the park that makes a lot of short visits (being a high earner it has a high forgone earnings component to its costs). Points **d**, **e** and **f** also represent households with the same costs per visit. Whereas both **d** and **e** make few visits, **d** does so because it has no attraction to the facilities offered, but **e** does so because it has access to another park close to its residential location. Household **f**, on the other hand, makes a lot of visits. Although it is identical to **e** in every other respect, it is not located close to another recreational area. It is clear from the above that if we are to trace out how a particular household, such as **a**, would react to changes in the cost per visit, then we need to group together households that are similar to **a**. The locus of points linking such households would then constitute their *demand curve* for the recreational facilities that the site has to offer. Similarity here means grouping our observations according to income, preference for recreation and access to other recreational facilities. Given the demand curves we can calculate the benefits of the site by taking the area under these curves. Adding up the consumer surpluses for different categories of households gives us the overall benefit of the site.

If the model developed here is to be used to evaluate the benefits of environmental *improvements*, then further work has to be done. It is no longer enough to separate out the groups according to what other recreational facilities they may have access to. We now need to know how much of the willingness to pay of a category of households will increase if the facility at a particular site is improved to allow, for example, the possibility of fishing in a lake where none was possible before. This in turn requires knowledge of how much of the willingness to pay for each site is due to each of its specific facilities. Then by looking across sites we will be able to trace out changes in this willingness to pay as facilities change. The data required for such an exercise would include the facilities of each site and the location of each household relative to all the sites. This is clearly a very large amount of information and so some simplifying assumptions will be necessary in many cases. What these are and how they affect the result is discussed later in this section. If we can derive the demand curve for recreation for a particular category of households defined by household characteristics such as income, education and the liking for recreational facilities, and we can show how this demand curve would shift if facilities improved, then the benefit of the improvement can be derived. Box 3.8 illustrates some results obtained by travel-cost approaches in comparison to contingent valuation.

Box 3.8   **A comparison of the simple travel cost and contingent valuation estimates of water-quality benefits**

	Water quality change		
	Loss of area	*Boatable to game fishing*	*Boatable to swimming*
Approach	(1981$)	(1981$)	(1981$)
Contingent valuation			
Direct question	19.71	21.18	31.18
	(17)	(17)	(17)
Payment card	19.71	30.88	51.18
	(17)	(17)	(17)
Iterative bidding ($25)	6.58	4.21	10.53
	(19)	(19)	(19)
Iterative bidding ($125)	36.25	20.13	48.75
	(16)	(16)	(16)
Simple travel cost	3.53	7.16	28.86
	(69)	(69)	(69)

The analysis relates to several sites at the Monongahela River basin in Pennsylvania. The water-quality changes involve (a) water-quality changes that would preclude all recreational use ("loss of area"), (b) improving water quality, and (c) improving to the level where swimming could occur. The two approaches (CVM and TCM) are seen to be broadly consistent. See V. K. Smith and W. Desvousges, *Measuring Water Quality Benefits* (Boston: Kluwer, 1987), pp. 170–74.

More on existence value

The introduction indicated that existence value is a value placed on an environmental good and which is *unrelated to any actual or potential use of the good*. At first sight this may seem an odd category of economic value, for, surely, value derives from use? To see how existence values can be positive, consider the many environmental funds and organisations in existence to protect endangered species. The subject of these campaigns could be a readily identifiable and used habitat near to the person support-ing the campaign. It is very often a remote environment, how-ever, so much so that it is not realistic to expect the campaigner to use it now, or even in the future. Many people none the

---

Box 3.9   **Membership of conservation and nature appreciation groups in the UK**

	1989
National Trust	1,700,000
Royal Society for the Protection of Birds	540,000
Greenpeace	282,000
Royal Society for Nature Conservation	204,000
Worldwide Fund for Nature	125,000
Friends of the Earth	100,000
Ramblers Association	70,800
Woodland Trust	62,000
Council for the Protection of Rural England	38,000
Men of the Trees	6,000
London Wildlife Trust	5,000
Soil Association	5,000
Marine Conservation Society	4,000
Flora and Fauna Preservation Society	3,500
British Association for Nature Conservation	900

Source: Susan Pearce, London Environmental Economics Centre

less support campaigns to protect tropical forests, to ban the hunting of whales, to protect giant pandas, rhinoceros, and so on. All are consumable vicariously through film and television, but vicarious demand cannot explain the substantial support for such campaigns and activities (see Box 3.9). This type of value, unrelated to use, is existence value.

Economists have suggested a number of motives, all of which reduce to some form of *altruism* – caring for other people or other beings:

(i) *Bequest* motives relate to the idea of willing a supply of natural environments to one's heirs or to future generations in general. It is no different to passing on accumulated personal assets. As noted above, however, we prefer to see bequest motives as part of a *use* value, the user being the heir or future generation. It is possible, of course, to think of a bequest as relating to the satisfaction that we believe will be given to future generations from the mere existence of the asset, but the very notion of bequest tends to imply that the inheritor makes some use of the asset;

(ii) *Gift* motives are very similar but the object of the gift tends to be a current person – a friend, say, or a relative. Once again, gift motives are more likely to be for use by the recipient. We do not therefore count the gift motive as explaining existence value – it is one more use value based on altruism.

(iii) *Sympathy* for people or animals. This motive is more relevant to existence value. Sympathy for animals tends to vary by culture and nation, but in a great many nations it is the norm, not the exception. It is consistent with this motive that we are willing to pay to preserve habitats out of sympathy for the sentient beings, including humans, that occupy them.

Much of the literature on existence value stops here. The reason for this is that altruistic motives are familiar to economists. They make economic analysis more complex but, by and large, altruism can be conveniently subsumed in the conventional model of rational economic behaviour. Essentially, it says that the wellbeing of one individual depends on the wellbeing of another individual. There may, however, be other motives at work. Existence values may, for example, reflect some judgement about the "rights" of other non-human beings, or a feeling of "stewardship" about the global or local environment.

Genuine motives for environmental concern are likely to be many and varied. For current purposes what matters is that economic valuation of environmental gains and losses needs to take account of those motives.

Empirical measures of option and existence value

It is possible to secure empirical estimates of option and existence value by the use of methods which adopt a *contingent valuation* approach. In this section we report several studies which have attempted to obtain actual measures.

David Brookshire, Larry Eubanks and Alan Randall measured the *option price* (option value plus expected consumer surplus) and *existence value* of grizzly bears and bighorn sheep in Wyoming, both species being subject to threats to their existence. By asking hunters for their WTP in a context where the probability of there being adequate supplies of these species was variable, the authors were able to uncover different types of economic value. A hunter who was certain of his own intentions none the less faced uncertain supply. The pattern of bids is shown in Box 3.10. The U refers to respondents who were uncertain if they would hunt, the C to respondents who were certain they would. This captures an element of demand uncertainty. The subscripts 5 and 15 refer to the number of years before a programme being hypothetically paid for by the licences for which the respondents were bidding.

The overall option price should increase as the probability of supply increases. This was the result predicted by the theory and it is seen to hold in this case. One might also expect the bids based on certain demand to exceed those based on uncertain demand, but the diagrams show that there is no systematic relationship. Respondents who indicated they would never hunt the bears or sheep were asked what they would none the less pay to preserve the species. They were further divided into

Box 3.10   **Option values and existence values**

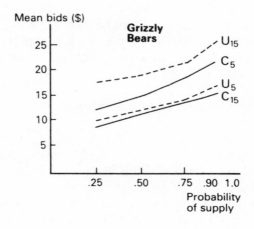

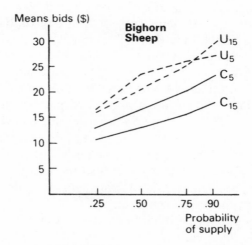

Mean grizzly and bighorn bids for certain (**C**) and uncertain (**U**) hunting demands over alternative time horizons (5 and 15 years).

Source: D. Brookshire, L. Eubanks and A. Randall, "Estimating option prices and existence values for wildlife resources", *Land Economics*, Vol. 9, no. 1, February 1983.

observers (a form of use value) and *non-observers* ("pure" existence value). The results provided estimates of "observer option price" – i.e. the option price associated with keeping the species for recreational observation – and existence value. The results were:

| | Bears | | Sheep | |
	5 years	15 years	5 years	15 years
Average observer option price ($)	21.8	21.0	23.0	18.0
Average existence value	24.0	15.2	7.4	6.9

Clearly, these are significant sums. To see this compare them to the average option prices for hunting under, say, 90 per cent probability of future supply. For grizzly bears and the 5-year time horizon the sequence would be $21.5 option hunting price compared to $21.8 option observer price and $24.0 for existence value. Average existence value is on a par with the bids to maintain the population for hunting and observation.

In a later paper, Brookshire *et al.*[1] detail findings relating to the Grand Canyon. By looking at the bids made by respondents to experience improved visibility (regardless of whether visits take place or not), the authors find that the total "preservation bid" for the Grand Canyon's visibility was $4.43 per month, compared to a "user bid" of $0.07 per month. Interpreting existence value as the difference between total preservation value and use value, the finding is thus that existence value dominates preservation in this case. Existence value stands in the ratio of 66:1 to user values. (Note that what is being preserved is visibility, not the site itself.) The explanation for such a large ratio is that the resource in question is unique – it has no substitutes. Where substitutes exist one would expect existence values to be lower, and this tends to be the picture in other studies on existence value.

Jon Strand [2] reports a CVM-type study of acid rain for Norway. After indicating the nature of the environmental problem – damage to freshwater fish from acid rain – respondents were given a starting-point figure for the global cost of stopping acid pollution which was translated into a special income tax. They were then asked if they were willing to pay this sum. The approach was thus of the "take-it-or-leave-it" kind rather than one involving iterative bids in which respondents could vary their bid according to different levels of clean-up. But the hypothetical tax rates were varied across the four samples of respondents interviewed – i.e. the tax rate was the same for each sample but varied between samples. The "yes" responses were found for the lower taxes. Strand then estimates "bid curves" using this information in a conditional probability framework – i.e. estimating the probability that a respondent would pay a particular tax given a certain income. Strand estimates that the average bid was 800 Norwegian Krone per capita. Given a population of 3.1 million, this translates to a "national" benefit of 2.5 billion Krone per annum. Earlier work by Strand suggests that user values are about 1 billion Krone, so that subtracting this from the implied total preservation value of 2.5 billion Krone gives an existence value of 1.5 billion Krone. In 1982 terms this translates to some $270 million per annum or about 1 per cent of the Norwegian GNP. Note that, by asking WTP, the Strand study probably underestimates the true value of benefits of reduced aquatic acidification. The reason for this is that a good deal of the acidity arises from "imported" pollution and respondents will generally have been aware of this. Accordingly, they may well have had the attitude that others besides themselves should pay for the clean-up.

Conclusions on valuing the environment

It is not essential to be persuaded that the monetary valuations illustrated in this chapter are "accurate". Economics is not, and cannot be, a science in the sense of a laboratory subject or an analysis of physical objects. Its laboratory, after all, is human society itself. What does matter is that the implications of the valuation procedures outlined here are understood. These are:

(i) By at least trying to put money values on some aspects of environmental quality we are underlining the fact that environmental services are *not* free. They do have values in the same sense as marketed goods and services have values. The absence of markets must not be allowed to disguise this important fact.

(ii) By trying to value environmental services we are forced into a rational decision-making frame of mind. Quite simply, we are forced to think about the gains and losses, the benefits and costs of what we do. If nothing else, economic valuation has made a great advance in that respect.

(iii) Many things *cannot* be valued in money terms. That is altogether different from saying they are "priceless" in the sense of having infinite values.

(iv) The fact that we find *positive* values for so many environmental functions means that an economic system which allocates resources according to economic values (i.e. consumer preferences) *must* take account of the positive economic values for environmental quality. Yet the actual values (as opposed to those imputed by the techniques discussed in this chapter) are zero in many cases. We return to this point in Chapter 7.

Notes

1. D. Brookshire, W. Schulze, M. Thayer, "Some unusual aspects of valuing a unique natural resource", mimeo, University of Wyoming, 1985.
2. J. Strand, "Valuation of fresh-water fish as a public food in Norway", Institute of Economics, Oslo University, mimeo, 1981.

ANNEX TO CHAPTER 3

The problem of extending valuation techniques and applying them across a wider range of values should not be under-estimated. Techniques vary in complexity, data are not always readily available, and there are sometimes considerable demands on both the practitioners and the recipients of such studies. The problems are set out below.[1]

1. The tables are adapted from David Miltz, *The Use of Benefits Estimation in Environmental Decision-Making*, Environment Directorate, OECD, Paris, October 1988.

Difficulties in the application of estimation techniques

Technique	Source of problem	Comment

DIRECT VALUATIONS

1. Hedonic pricing	Data problems	Specialized skills required
	Identification of the independent variables	Differences in residential property prices can be attributed to a host of different variables. In order to pick up the effects on the price of housing, all significant variables must be identified. Bias can result from the exclusion of relevant variables and unreliable estimates may result where irrelevant variables are included.
	Measurement and data procurement	Measurement and data procure-ment problems abound for this technique, especially when applied outside the USA. Housing

Technique	Source of problem	Comment
		prices, the dependent variable, are not readily accessible in many countries, e.g. the UK. Measurement of pollution levels also presents many problems.
Mathematical and statistical difficulties		
	Choice of the functional form	Clear guidelines do not exist for the choice of the functional form relating the dependent variable to the independent variables. The judgement of the practitioner is required. The form selected has a significant impact on the inferred benefit of pollution abatement.
	Correlation of the pollution variables	Measures of pollution are highly correlated, e.g. suspended particles and nitrogen dioxide. In practice aggregate or proxy variables are used. The results of the hedonic process are highly sensitive to this exercise.
Economic assumptions and interpretations		
	Fixed supply of housing units	The supply of housing units may vary from being fixed to being responsive to price changes. The typical assumption of a fixed supply is questionable.
	Assumption of equilibrium	In many countries the housing market is not efficient, e.g. as a

Technique	Source of problem	Comment
		result of public sector rationing and the sequential bidding procedure typical in house sales. The implications of these inefficiencies on the model results are not clear.
	Market segmentation	Market segmentation presents a problem in that mobility between locales may be poor. Pooling of such data may result in bias.
	Mitigating behaviour	Pollution effects may be avoided by measures other than moving location. Where mitigating behaviour involves modifications to the housing unit, information on housing attributes is required to value pollution costs. This detailed information is seldom available.
	Inter-pretation of results	The precise interpretation of the willingness-to-pay measure for pollution reduction is unclear. The extent to which perception of the pollution risk to health affects the valuation and the degree to which biases may result from expectations of future pollution are not clear.
	Accuracy and reliability	The degree of accuracy of the analysis is questionable, with estimated costs of pollution being out by an order of magnitude.

Technique	Source of problem	Comment
2. Wage risk studies	**Data/statistical issues**	**Specialized skills required**
	Measurement and data procurement	Wage studies do not usually suffer from the same data procurement problems as hedonic house price studies. Concerns regarding the identification of the independent variables are, however, similar.
	Mathematical and statistical difficulties	
	Risk	A great deal has been written about the problem of valuing a life given low probabilities of death. The problem relates primarily to the difficulty in perception between a statistical death or accident rate of, say, 1 in 200,000 as compared with 1 in 250,000. Also, different individuals have different attitudes to risk, for example some may be risk-averse while others may enjoy taking risks.
	Economic assumptions and inter-pretations	
	Market assumptions	The reliability with which the hedonic approach can measure wage-risk premia depends on the reasonability of the assumption that labour markets are free and that individuals correctly perceive

Technique	Source of problem	Comment
		risk. The pervasive presence of trade unions in many OECD member countries suggests that, depending on trade union power, wage differentials may not readily reflect environmental risk.
	Accuracy and reliability	Overviews of the wage risk studies reveal wide discrepancies in the values placed on a life. Even negative coefficients on risk have been reported.
3. Contingent valuation method (CVM)	**Data problems**	**Intermediate skills required**
	Bias ●Strategic ●Design ●Hypothetical ●Operational	A major problem for the CVM is in the eliciting of unbiased responses to the highly structured hypothetical markets. Strategic bias, i.e. the incentive to "free-ride", does not appear to be significant. Design bias derives from the information presented to the respondent, the sequence of presentation, the bidding instrument and the starting point of such bidding. The alternative designs of the hypothetical market have been shown to influence, or bias, the CVM valuations. Hypothetical bias measures the influence of an artificial as against an actual market on the valuations. Operational bias results from differences in the conditions between the actual and hypothetical markets.

Technique	Source of problem	Comment
	Economic assumptions and interpretations	
	WTP *vs* WTA	A debate continues with regard to the observed empirical asymmetry, multiples of 3 are common, between these two benefit measures. Conventional economic wisdom posits that an individual should be indifferent between an amount received or paid for marginal deteriorations or improvements in environmental quality respectively. Much more work is required to adequately explain this variability.
	Accuracy and Reliability	CVM presents a highly flexible framework for the valuation of almost all environmental benefits. A comparison of CVM results with those of other techniques reveals an accuracy range of $+/-60$ per cent. As noted above, problems persist in reconciling WTP and WTA measures.
4. Travel cost method (TCM)	**Data problems**	**Intermediate skills required**
	Large data requirements	This technique requires a large quantity of data which can be very expensive to collect, and collate. In order to value the benefits of environmental improvement it is necessary to know how much the willingness-to-pay, for a particular stratification of households, will

Technique	Source of problem	Comment
		change for a given change in the supply of amenities at a given site.
	Data on travel costs and travel times	The cost of visiting an area includes the transportation costs and the opportunity cost of travel time. Time spent at the site also involves an element of opportunity cost. Significant biases may result from using incorrect values of these very difficult-to-measure costs.
	Household characteristics	Hourly wage rates are rarely available. A hedonic wage equation must therefore be used to estimate this wage rate to allow a calculation of travel costs. Much information, e.g. education, must be obtained. Many statistical problems are inherent in providing a good hedonic wage equation.
	Site variables	Data on recreation site facilities require careful measurement and selection of these descriptions of site characteristics and quality.
	Economic assumptions and inter- pretation	
	Single purpose visits	It is assumed that travel is undertaken solely for the purpose of visiting the site. Where visits are multi-purpose the costs may have to be divided in an arbitrary manner and the accuracy of the results may be seriously affected.

Technique	Source of problem	Comment
	Mathematical and statistical difficulties	
	Specification of the demand equation	Difficulties in establishing the statistical form of the demand function require that the practitioner use professional judgement in selecting the best form, e.g. linear. Inadequate specifications may result in poor benefit estimates.
	Discrete nature of the problem	The use of discrete multi-valued data, i.e. the number of visits, in estimation procedures is problematical.
	Economic assumptions and inter-pretations	
	Truncation bias	Truncation bias may present TCM with a serious difficulty. It relates to the problem of ignoring non-visitors to the site. If the cost per visit were lowered or the quality of amenities improved some of these non-visitors would frequent the site. A great difficulty exists in tracing these individuals and in ascertaining the extent of possible truncation bias.
	Accuracy and reliability	TCM is a useful technique where adequate data is available and where some of the above concerns do not blur the accuracy of the

Technique	*Source of problem*	*Comment*

results. Comparisons of results with the CVM reveals that results of two methods fall within a range of +/− 60 per cent.

INDIRECT VALUATIONS

Data problems

	Measurement and data procurement	Indirect valuations involve the identification of a dose-response relationship. This technical relationship typically requires accurate measures of ambient pollution levels. Accounting for variations presents some problems. Large quantities of data are usually required. For example, macroepidemiological studies which try to establish a relationship between morbidity, mortality, and pollution levels, require that a large data base of socio-economic and pollution variables are regressed against morbidity and mortality statistics.
	Mathematical and statistical problems	
	Controlling for extraneous variables	Observations are frequently made in real life settings, e.g. the corrosion of outdoor materials. Problems arise in trying to identify and isolate the independent variables. For example, the major problem in trying to establish a relationship between pollution

Technique	Source of problem	Comment
		concentration and material damage are: some chemicals only react at threshold levels, some chemicals may interact, the effects of microclimates make different locations difficult to compare, laboratory findings do not adequately mirror the real-world findings.
	Identifying the functional form	The functional form of the dose-response relationship is very difficult to specify. Incorrect specifications could result in poor estimates of damage functions when applying a valuation technique.
	Economic assumptions and inter-pretations	
	Inadequate number of studies	Many dose-response relationships have not been adequately studied. For example, in the case of materials corrosion, much of the technical literature in this area has been financed by private industry and commercial interest has dictated which materials were investigated.
	Averting behaviour	Behavioural considerations are important for reliable dose-response relationships. In the case of medical care averting behaviour may involve investment in preventative medical care or, in the case of household soiling,

Technique	Source of problem	Comment
		averting behaviour may involve regular cleaning operations or investment in air filters.
	Accuracy and reliability	The accuracy of these technical relationships depends on the extent to which stochastic and localized elements can be accounted for, the current understanding of the physical process and the degree of investment in trying to unravel the particular dose-response relationship.

4. ACCOUNTING FOR THE ENVIRONMENT

If an effective management of the natural and environmental and resource base is to be achieved, policy makers need to have access to a consistent, reliable and comparable data set, relating to the availability and use of such resources. Such information is gathered with increasing frequency at the national and international level and it would be difficult to overestimate the importance of these endeavours. One special approach, which is part of this exercise, is an attempt to present the relevant information within an accounting framework.

As with all accounting systems, the objective of environmental accounting is to:

(i) prepare a "balance sheet" giving a profile of what *stocks* of the resource are available at a given point in time,

(ii) prepare an account of what *uses* are made of these stocks, what *sources* they are derived from and how they are added to or transformed over time, and,

(iii) ensure that the *stock accounts* and the *flow accounts* are consistent, so that the balance sheet in any year can be derived from the balance sheet of the previous year plus the flow accounts of that year.

In this chapter we examine the substantial effort that has gone into the preparation of various kinds of environmental accounts, essentially over the last fifteen years. Different approaches are reviewed and their relevance, if any, to the British system of dealing with environmental data is examined.

The attempts to incorporate environmental issues within some accounting system can be traced back, on the one hand to the work of Nordhaus and Tobin (1972) in the United States, and on the other to the natural resource accounting modelling work of the Norwegian government beginning around 1974 (OECD, 1988). Each of these represents a distinct approach that has been followed by others subsequently, and with considerable modifications. However, the essential distinction between the two approaches remains fairly clear. Whereas Nordhaus and Tobin attempted to incorporate environmental considerations into the existing national accounts, the Norwegian approach (and subsequently that of the French and Canadian governments) has been to develop the accounts for the natural and environmental resources in a separate physical accounting framework.

Although we naturally think of "accounts" in money terms, there is in fact no reason why such accounts should not be presented in physical units, as long as they present the stocks and flows in a clear identifiable way and as long as they achieve the reconciliation between the sets of stock and flow accounts as described above. For example, energy balance sheets can and have been prepared, with sectoral sources and uses of energy being presented in physical terms (e.g. tonnes of oil, equivalent or tetra joules). See, for example, the *Digest of United Kingdom Energy Statistics* for such a set of balances. There are advantages and disadvantages to each approach, and these can best been seen after each of them has been described, and some of the applications of the accounts considered.

In the next two sections (pp.95-113), the physical and monetary accounts approaches respectively are described and evaluated in greater detail. Special attention is paid to specific applications, including those of Norway and France for the physical accounting systems and those of Japan and Indonesia for the monetary accounting systems. In the fourth section (p.113) a comparative evaluation of the two approaches is made. This takes into account the findings of various review meetings on environmental accounting organized by UNEP, the UNSO and the World Bank. The fifth section (p.116) describes the current treatment of environmental issues in the British accounting system and the final section considers what lessons can be learnt from the experiences of other countries with regard to the development of environmental accounting in the United Kingdom.

Environmental accounting: the physical approach

The "physical" approach was pioneered by the Norwegian government, which set up, in 1974, a Department of Natural Resources to develop and introduce a system of natural resource accounting and budgeting. In 1978, the French government decided to introduce in a phased way a system of natural resource accounts, and set up the Commission Interministérielle des Comptes du Patrimonie Naturel for this purpose. More recently, the Canadian government has begun to develop a similar system of accounts (Friend, 1986) and there is currently a UNEP proposal under way to initiate a system of physical accounts in three developing countries. The essential features of the approach can best be seen by looking in some detail at the actual systems developed in Norway and France.

Box 4.1 **Classification of resources in the Norwegian accounting system**

Resource	*Physical Classification*
Material	Minerals: minerals, hydrocarbons, stone gravel and sand.
	Biological resources: in the air, water, on land and in the ground.
	Inflowing resources: solar radiation, hydrological cycle, wind, ocean currents.
Environmental	Status resources: air, water, soil and space.

The Norwegian accounting system

The Norwegian accounting system divides resources into two broad categories: material resources and environmental resources. Within each, the classification is as shown in Box 4.1. Note that some resources, e.g. water, appear both as material resources (such as hydro-power) and as environmental (such as water quality for recreation, drinking etc.). The units in which the resources are measured and the quality of data will naturally vary according the item being considered. For the mineral stock accounts (principally gas and oil) the following categories are defined: developed reserves, undeveloped reserves, new fields, revaluation and extraction, all measured in physical units suitable to the item in question. Reserves are considered developed when most of the basic investment has been made and ordinary production started. Revaluation arises when previous estimates are revised. Corresponding to the stock accounts for these items there are flow accounts that trace the amounts extracted, plus what is imported into various end uses, such as industry (by sector), households, government and exports. For biological resources, principally fish, the categories are: reserves, recruitment, revaluation, extraction and natural mortality. All are self-explanatory, except perhaps recruitment, which represents new additions to the stock. For biological resources a breakdown by geographical location is often important and is therefore undertaken. For inflowing resources (the remaining item under material resources) no accounts appear to have been prepared.

The accounts for the material resources have proved easier to prepare than those for the environmental resources. In the case of the latter the issue of quality is clearly important and so far a number of questions remain unanswered. These accounts consist of two parts: an *emissions account* which deals with the emissions of waste products into the air, water and land; and a *state account*, which describes the state of the environment at different points in time and changes in the environment in the periods between them. An important feature of these accounts is the geographical dimension. The emissions records for air pollution show, for example, emissions of different gases by sector and region. An illustration of the state and emission accounts would be: those for land which give a breakdown of land by end use (agricultural, forest, other unbuilt, residential and other built) for different regions. The corresponding flow accounts show the shift from one category to another over time. An example of the sort of data that is included in these accounts is given in Box 4.2.

Box 4.2   **Land use accounts in Norway** (hectares)

Period	Land use after development	Total	Land developed Agri-culture	Forest	Other unbuilt
1955–65	Total	17322	6294	5785	5243
	Residential	10852	4078	4085	2689
	Other built-up	6470	2216	1700	2554
1965–75	Total	21531	6842	8462	6227
	Residential	12771	3989	5789	2993
	Other built-up	8760	2853	2673	3234

Emission Accounts in Norway (Tonnes)

	Sulphur dioxide 1980	1982	Nitrogen oxide 1980	1982	Carbon monoxide 1980	1982
Total	140	112	134	120	582	643
Agriculture	2	2	2	3	19	21
Manufacturing	108	84	30	20	34	68
Transport	11	11	38	37	35	40
Households	6	5	28	29	390	407

What has been achieved as a result of establishing these basic accounts? The data collected in this exercise have been used to prepare forecasts of future use of natural resources and their implied environmental impacts. These forecasts are referred to as "resource budgets" and it is clear that they have been more successfully completed for some of the resources

Box 4.3   **French and Norwegian accounting classifications**

French classification	Norwegian classification
1. Type of environment Inland waters Air Soil	Environmental resources Water Air Soil
2. Living organisms Fauna Flora	2. Biological resources
3. Land Unbuilt areas	3. Land resources
4. Underground resources Mineral and energy resources	4. Mineral resources

than others. In a recent review of the Norwegian accounting experience OECD (1988), the author has indicated mixed results.

The most successful application has been in the preparation of a set of energy accounts, where the natural resource accounts provide an input into the energy demand forecasting model and energy policy debate as well as the model forecasting emissions of major air pollutants that are the outcome of the energy mix that is chosen. Some success has also been claimed for the land use accounts. These are said to be of considerable benefit for the physical planning of land use as well as its better coordination at the local (municipal) and county level. On the other hand, the accounts on fisheries have proved to be disappointing and those of forests and mineral resources have had little impact. At a more general level, the whole exercise is viewed as beneficial in terms of improving understanding and raising knowledge of environmental problems.

Resource accounting in France
The French system is built on similar lines to the Norwegian as far as the categories are concerned. Box 4.3 shows the relationship between the two sets of classifications and it can be seen there is a great deal of similarity. However, the two systems differ in the way they construct the accounts for each of the categories. The French system defines the following categories: *central accounts* that describe the state of the resource and variations in it between the beginning and the end of the period; *peripheral accounts* that show the relationship between one resource and another and between human activities and the resource under consideration; and *agent accounts* that describe the flows between the resource and an economic activity, in terms of physical quantities, "*as well as the expenditures approved for [its] maintenance, repair, supervision or development*" (Cornière, 1986). Thus we see that the French system is both more ambitious and more comprehensive than the Norwegian and includes some monetary valuations as part of the picture. Box 4.4 gives a schematic representation of the full set of natural resource accounts for the French system as well as its intended linkages with the economic and other accounts. A particular representation of one set of accounts, i.e. the water accounts, is given in Box 4.5, with each of the three types – central, peripheral and agent accounts – being illustrated.

A full appraisal of the French system has not been undertaken as yet. While the above accounts certainly present useful information on the state and use of natural resources in the country, its use in planning and policy analysis has yet to be demonstrated.

Overall these two sets of accounts demonstrate some interesting aspects of the environmental profile of the countries concerned. They also show some linkages between the environment and the economy that are of general interest. However, the use to which these can be put, in terms of economic analysis that has policy relevance, is unclear. Hence, at this stage we would not recommend that the UK proceed along the path of developing a system of physical resource accounts similar to those undertaken in Norway or France. The issues involved are discussed further

Box 4.4   Structure of the natural resource accounts system in France

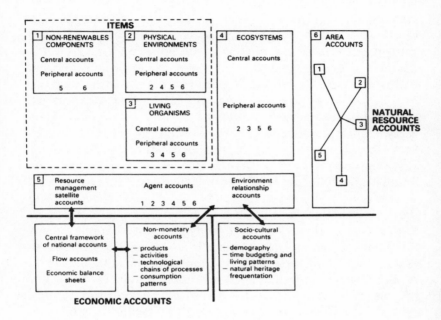

KEY: 1 — Stock at the beginning of the period
2 — Upward adjustment in known reserves
3 — Downward adjustment in known reserves
4 — Gross natural increase
5 — Natural depletion
6 — Increase due to resource development
7 — Depletion due to withdrawal
8 — Imports

Source: Cornière, 1986.

Box 4.5 **Central account of water in France** (billions of cubic meters)

Beginning of period

Sub-items	I	II	III	IV	Total
Long term					
1. Snow and glaciers	130				130
Groundwaters					
2. Ground aquifers	300	200	100		600
3. Alluvial aquifers	100	250	300	50	709
3. Confined aquifers	200				200
Medium term					
5. Lakes and ponds	10	15	15		30
6. Dams		8			8
Short term					
7. Rivers	21	23	53	68	165
11. Human activities	2				2
TOTAL					1844

End of period

Sub-items	I	II	III	IV	Total
Long term					
1. Snow and glaciers	150				150
Groundwaters					
2. Ground aquifers	350	150	70	20	585
3. Alluvial aquifers	90	240	320	73	723
3. Confined aquifers	200				200
Medium term					
5. Lakes and ponds	15	15	10		30
6. Dams		8			8
Short term					
7. Rivers	20	25	36	60	133
11. Human activities				2	2
12. External					13
TOTAL					1844

Source: Cornière, 1986.

Table 4.5 (contd.)   **Peripheral accounts of water in France** (billions of cubic meters)

Origins			*Destinations*	
Evaporation from the Sea		209	Runoff	165
Evapo-transpiration			Percolation	90
of which:	Plants	166	Infiltration	117
	Soil	59	Interception	68
	Air	6		
		440		440

The above table describes the exchanges between natural elements: soil, air, living organisms and seawater. It is an account showing interdependence of the elements with respect to water. In a general system of natural resource accounting the figures are the starting point for bridges linking one element (water in this case) with the others. An example is the amount of water withdrawn or returned by man.

Operating account (billions of cubic meters)

	Withdrawn	*Return*	*Evaporation or net consumption*
Urban population	5.7	4.5	1.2
Industry	4.6	4.2	0.4
Agriculture	7.6	2.1	5.5
Power stations	16.0	15.4	0.6
TOTAL	33.9	26.2	7.7

The volume returned is less than that withdrawn, since part of the water has been transformed into stream or vapour (industry, power stations, urban population) or infiltrated directly into the ground (and used, for example, by agriculture).

Source: Cornière, 1986.

Box 4.5 (contd.) **Agent/evaluation accounts of water in France** (millions of francs)

Consolidated expenditure	Total	Consolidated income	Total
Operating expenditure	17161	Sales of goods and services	21477 3151
Current outward transfers	1343	Financing from	
Gross saving transfers	13500	current inward transfers	7311
Total current expenditure	32004	Total current income	32004
Investment	13893 440	Limited savings	13500
Net flow of financial assets	807	Net flow of financial liabilities	1700
Total capital expenditure	14700	Total capital income	14700

National expenditure by function (millions of francs)

	Investment	Operation	Total
Treatment, non-connected industries	765	1500	2265
Drainage and treatment, local communities	6230	6000	12230
Supply of drinking water	4987	8850	13837
Agricultural water	1390	350	1740
Water control	513	300	813
TOTAL	13885	17000	30885

Source: Cornière, 1986.

Box 4.5 (contd.)   **Water quality balance sheet** (in billions of cubic meters)

River basin	Quality levels (present status)				Total	Quality objectives				Total
	1	**2**	**3**	**4**		**1**	**2**	**3**	**4**	
Ardour-Garonne	7	6	14	13	40	10	7	11	12	40
Artois-Picardy	–	–	2	2	4	2	1	1	–	4
Loire-Brittany	6	5	11	13	35	9	7	9	10	35
Rhine-Meuse	1	2	4	6	13	4	3	3	3	13
Rhone-Mediterranean	6	8	16	25	55	15	11	12	17	55
Seine-Normandy	1	2	6	9	18	8	4	3	3	18
Total (whole country)	21	23	53	68	165	48	33	39	45	165

Quality 1 is the highest and quality 4 is the lowest.

Source: Cornière, 1986.

after we have considered the monetary approach to environmental accounting.

Environmental accounting: the monetary approach

The monetary approach to environmental accounting attempts to link the use of environmental resources to the national income accounts. Such accounts are intended to value the goods and services produced within an economy in a given period of time and, although they have only been in existence for around fifty years, they have a central place in the evaluation of economic performance and the design of economic policy, both at the microeconomic and the macroeconomic level. However, it has long been recognized that the methods by which these accounts are constructed, which has been standardized by the United Nations as the system of national accounts (UN, 1968), fails to measure certain aspects of "valuable" production in the economy correctly and overestimates the benefits of other kinds of valuation.

As far as the environment is concerned, the main areas of measurement error in the monetary national accounts are:

(i) the use of defensive expenditures,
(ii) the negative impact of any environmental damage on the economic welfare of the society, and,
(iii) the treatment of degradation or depreciation of natural and environmental resources.
Each of these is discussed in detail below.

Defensive expenditures
The national accounts attempt to measure the value of goods and services produced in the economy. Valuation here is based on the notion of individual and collective utility or welfare and so the ultimate purpose of these accounts is to measure the *welfare* of the individuals that comprise the economic structure under consideration. In an immediate sense this value is obtained by looking not at national income but at those components of it that impinge directly on human welfare. In particular, the portion of national income that is saved but not consumed does not affect *current* welfare. Equally, it could be argued that expenditures by households to protect themselves against the adverse consequences of the production process – air and water pollution, noise nuisance, etc. – are properly regarded as costs of producing the goods and services that individuals enjoy and should therefore not be included as final expenditures giving rise to utility. If I double glaze my house when there is an increase in road traffic in the street, the expenditure incurred as a result does not raise my welfare relative to what it was, but only helps me to return to the level I enjoyed prior to the traffic increase. As measured, national income would show an increase when this expenditure was undertaken. As a measure of welfare change, however, that would be incorrect. Such expenditures to mitigate the impacts of environmental damage are referred to as *defensive expenditures*. For firms the treatment of defensive expenditures is more complex. In general, they are treated as intermediate expenditures – the costs of producing goods and services – and therefore do not appear in the final measure

of GDP. However, there can be cases where they appear as part of final value added, in which case they need to be corrected for in the same way as the household defensive expenditures.

The negative impact of environmental degradation

In addition to correcting national income for savings and defensive expenditures, measuring current welfare requires an estimate of the actual pollution that is generated but not mitigated – i.e. the "residual pollution damage". This clearly has an impact on the welfare of the society but is not accounted for in the traditional accounts. We can summarize the adjustments to national income accounts to obtain current welfare as:

CURRENT WELFARE = MEASURED CONSUMPTION − HOUSEHOLD
DEFENSIVE EXPENDITURES − MONETARY
VALUE OF RESIDUAL POLLUTION DAMAGE

The treatment of capital depreciation

What is of interest as far as this document is concerned, however, is not *current* welfare but a measure of the economy's *potential* welfare, or the expected welfare of its members over a long (perhaps indefinite) period of time. In this regard, it has been shown theoretically that, *as long as markets operate freely and efficiently*, measured national income, appropriately adjusted for defensive expenditures, is the proper measure of present and future welfare in that society (Mirrlees, 1969; Weitzman, 1976). The basic notion is that GNP equals consumption which represents current welfare, plus investment which equals the present value of future consumption, both in the absence of market failure. The absence of market failure means that in *all* markets and for *all* commodities prices must equal the *marginal social costs of production* (see Chapter 7).

However, we know that markets are not perfect, and so the question arises, how should measured national income be adjusted to obtain a measure of society's long-run welfare? In order to do this it is necessary, in addition to the adjustments identified above, to look at the way the economy is accumulating and decumulating its physical and environmental capital.

We ignore issues relating to man-made capital, as they are not central to questions of adjustments arising from environmental concerns. As far as environmental capital is concerned, we need to distinguish between exhaustible resources, renewable resources and eco-systems that are essential for economic activity.

For exhaustible resources, it has been shown that if the resource is being depleted too fast then the current GNP is an overestimate of discounted long-run welfare, and should be adjusted downward (Devarajan and Weiner, 1988). On the other hand if it is being depleted too slowly, the reverse is the case.

The terms "too fast" and "too slow" can be made precise and quantified but this requires, *inter alia*, assumptions about the underlying discount rate and changes in the productive nature of the economy, both of which are matters of debate and uncertainty.

The same applies to renewable resources: non-optimal rates of extraction imply an overvaluation of current GNP. In this case the definition of optimality is even more complex and difficult to achieve.

Finally there is the use or abuse of land and ecosystems that can act as limits to the ultimate productive capacity of the economy. The implications of *ecosystem* degradation on GNP as a long-run measure have not been worked out fully but there is strong presumption that if it is being fundamentally degraded then current GNP is an overestimate of future GNP.

Sustainable income
The notion of "long-run discounted welfare" which has been developed above is related to, but not the same as, another notion that has been much discussed in recent times, and that is the concept of *sustainable income*.

Instead of attempting to measure the discounted welfare of the economy, it is argued that we should measure income as the flow of goods and services that the economy could generate *without reducing its productive capacity – i.e. the income that it could produce indefinitely*.

In order to calculate such an figure, which was initially proposed as a definition of income by Hicks (1946), one needs to subtract from GNP the depreciation in the physical and environmental capital that has taken place. This amounts to working with a net income measure. Although, the relationship between this measure, and current or long-term economic welfare has not been worked out so far, it is an attractive notion to work with for a number of reasons.

The notion of sustainable income captures the idea of a constant capital stock – both physical and environmental – that is at the heart of much of the discussion on sustainable development (see Chapter 2). Second, by looking at net income one is properly penalizing those economies that are generating a high current income by "selling off the family silver" – i.e. running down their capital stock. Third, even if sustainable income is not the same as long-term welfare for dynamic reasons, the construction of a measure of the latter is likely to be so complicated that it will never be implementable.

For all these reasons then we would support the measurement of *sustainable income*, with the adjustments for environmental degradation and costs of mitigation included as they were for the current measure of welfare. We have then:

SUSTAINABLE INCOME = MEASURED INCOME − HOUSEHOLD DEFENSIVE EXPENDITURES − MONETARY VALUE OF RESIDUAL POLLUTION − DEPRECIATION OF MAN-MADE CAPITAL − DEPRECIATION OF ENVIRONMENTAL CAPITAL (ECOSYSTEM FUNCTION DAMAGE, RENEWABLE CAPITAL, EXHAUSTIBLE CAPITAL)

The measures of physical and environmental capital are referred to separately because the ways in which they would be calculated could be very different, and to indicate that they are not entirely substitutable, one for the other.

In the remainder of this section we look at how adjustments to national accounts are actually made in specific cases and evaluate how effective they are in achieving the goals of measuring current welfare or sustainable income.

Measuring current income with environmental considerations: the case of Japan

In 1973 the Japanese government announced its first measures of Net National Welfare (NNW), which corrected National Income figures for a variety of factors, including environmental ones. These corrections drew quite heavily on the Measures of Economic Welfare concept proposed by Nordhaus and Tobin in 1972. A summary can be found in Uno (1988). The environmental adjustments were made on the following basis: for each of the main problems areas (water contamination, air pollution and waste disposal) a quality standard was established. The extent to which current emissions were in excess of the standard was then estimated and a removal cost calculated to restore pollution to the required standard. The implied losses due to environmental pollution are given in Box 4.6 (taken from Uno, 1988), along with other adjustments and the NNW and GNP totals. The adjusted value of GNP is referred to as NNW and appears as the penultimate row. The uncorrected value of GNP is given in the final row. Note that the adjustment is quite dramatic. Instead of "GNP" growing by a factor of 8.3 between 1955 and 1985, the adjusted measure suggests growth by a factor of 5.8 only.

There are three difficulties with this method of correction for environmental pollution. First, the choice of standard is arbitrary, although it may have a political basis. By choosing a low enough standard the costs can be made negligible and by choosing a high enough one they can be made astronomic. Related to this is the second point, which is that we are ignoring the impacts of any residual pollution that is left once the standard has been imposed. Unless this standard is optimal in a rather specific sense, some additional impact should be allowed for. The third point is that the approach ignores totally the impact of defensive expenditures, which should be allowed

Box 4.6   **Adjustments to GNP in Japan to obtain net national welfare (unit: billion yen, 1970 prices)**

Fiscal year	1955	1960	1965	1970	1975	1980	1985
NNW government expenditure	1,199	1,374	2,254	2,988	3,865	4,283	4,887
NNW personal consumption	10,427	14,706	22,168	32,097	43,003	54,009	61,700
Government capital service	62	99	169	317	559	756	1,103
Personal durable goods service	91	195	755	2,342	4,187	5,270	6,813
Leisure time	4,871	6,098	7,325	10,509	16,759	18,961	20,816
Extra-market activities	1,876	2,388	4,068	7,213	12,707	12,571	13,079
Environmental pollution (deduction)	-38	-1,037	-3,735	-6,805	-5,729	-3,932	-3,103
Loss due to urbanization (deduction)	-452	-695	-889	-1,113	-1,119	-1,272	-1,514
NNW	18,036	23,128	32,116	47,548	74,231	90,646	103,781
GNP	17,268	26,183	41,591	72,144	93,260	118,105	143,387

Source: Uno, 1988.

for if a correct measure is to be obtained. The problems with defensive expenditures are (a) it is difficult to isolate those items that fall specifically in this category and (b) there is always a danger of double counting if such expenditures also result in increased values for household and land services. There is a considerable literature on defensive expenditures and valuing residual pollution, but no effort has been made to attempt such a valuation on a national scale.

Natural resource accounts and the measurement of sustainable income: an illustration from Indonesia
If the objective is to obtain a measure of sustainable income, it is necessary to allow for any depletion of the capital stock of the country – either natural or man-made.

At present, if an entire forest is logged and the resulting revenues invested in a cement factory, national income would show a rise because of the investment in the cement factory *and* it would show a rise because of the logging activities. This, however, is a misrepresentation of the sustainable income level because it fails to allow for the decline in one productive asset (forests) while allowing for the increase in another asset (factories). As currently constituted, the United Nations SNA does not fully allow for changes in the natural asset base over time. There are no investment or depreciation entries for growth in renewable resources such as forests and fisheries; or for discoveries such as new oil fields; or for depletion in the asset base in both cases. However, any productive activities relating to these assets are included. The UN has approved the accounting of natural assets in the accounting framework but the method by which depletion or accretion should be allowed for has not been agreed upon.

The issues arising over how to adjust for changes in the natural asset base are illustrated in Box 4.7 by an example taken from Repetto *et al.* (1989), for forest resources. In physical units the opening stock of 100 is increased through discoveries, revisions etc. and subtracted from because of production, deforestation and degradation. As a result one arrives at the closing stock figure 85. However, for accounting purposes this change has to

Box 4.7   **Sample forestry accounts**

	Physical units	Unit value	Value (£)	Basis of calculation
Opening stock	100	1.00	100	
Additions:				
Discoveries	20	1.60	32	
Revisions	(30)	1.60	(48)	
Extensions	15	1.60	24	
Growth	0	1.60	0	
Reproduction	0	1.60	0	
Reductions:				
Production	(20)	1.60	(32)	
Deforestation	0	1.60	0	
Degradation	0	1.60	0	
Net change	(15)	1.60	(24)	
Revaluations:				
Opening stock	–	–	200	$100^x(£3-£1)$
Transactions	–	–	(21)	$15^x(£3-£1.6)$
Closing stock	85	3.00	255	

Source: Repetto *et al.*, 1989.

be included in value terms. Hence the unit value, or "rent" of the stock (i.e the price less costs incurred in extraction or production) is relevant. In the example, this unit value is assumed to be £1 at the beginning of the period, £3 at the end of the period and £1.6 on average over the whole period. As far as the national asset balance sheet is concerned, the change in net wealth is the difference between the value of the asset at the end of the period and at the beginning of the period, i.e. £255 − £100 = £155. The corresponding adjustment to Net National Product (which is the net of depreciation version of GNP) is less clear.

(i) One approach could be to increase NNP by £155, on the basis that all net additions to wealth are in fact income. However, this would lead to massive fluctuations in measured national income, particularly for countries where the natural asset base was subject to large variations in price (e.g. the oil-producing countries).

(ii) A second approach could be to allow only for the physical depletion in the resource base. In this example, this amounts to 20 units. Taking an average price for the units of £1.6 yields a reduction in NNP of £32.

(iii) A third approach would be to allow for physical depletion as well as any net additions. This would result in a net reduction of 15 units, which at average price of £1.6 per unit implies a reduction in NNP of $15 \times £1.6 = £24$. The United Nations (1977, 1980) has recommended that all changes in asset values be reflected in balance sheets and reconciliation accounts and not used to adjust GNP and calculate NNP. Repetto *et al.* and others have argued, however, that some adjustment to the national accounts is warranted on the grounds that without it reported income can be seriously misleading as an indicator of sustainable income. They propose the third of the above adjust-ments, referred to as the *net price method*. At the same time any revaluation to the stock is recorded in a separate revaluation reserve.

The application of this method to Indonesian petroleum, for-est and soil assets has been carried out by Repetto *et al.* (1989) and the implied adjustments to gross domestic product (GDP) are shown in Box 4.8. It can be seen that adjusted GDP is higher than actual GDP prior to 1974 and is lower thereafter, with the gap in 1984 being 17 per cent.

Environmental accounting: a physical or monetary approach?

So far we have examined two ways of dealing with environmen-tal accounts: a physical approach and a monetary approach. The physical approach has the advantage that it is easier to imple-ment and is not based on economic assumptions about valuation that could be invalid. In particular it is necessary that the prices

Box 4.8   **Comparison of GDP and "NDP"* in 1973 Rupiah (billions)**

Year	GDP[1]	Net change in natural resource sectors[2]			Soil	Net change	NDP
		Petroleum	Forestry				
1971	5,545	1,527	–312	–89	1,126	6,671
1972	6,067	337	–354	–83	–100	5,967
1973	6,753	407	–591	–95	–279	6,474
1974	7,296	3,228	–533	–90	2,605	9,901
1975	7,631	–787	–249	–85	–1,121	6,510
1976	8,156	–187	–423	–74	–684	7,472
1977	8,882	–1,225	–405	–81	–1,711	7,171
1978	9,567	–1,117	–401	–89	–1,607	7,960
1979	10,165	–1,200	–946	–73	–2,219	7,946
1980	11,169	–1,633	–965	–65	–2,663	8,506
1981	12,055	–1,552	–595	–68	–2,215	9,840
1982	12,325	–1,158	–551	–55	–1,764	10,561
1983	12,842	–1,825	–974	–71	–2,870	9,972
1984	13,520	–1,765	–493	–76	–2,334	11,186
Average annual growth	7.1%					4.0%

* Net domestic product, i.e. GDP – "net change".
1. In constant 1973 Rupiah, billions. From the Indonesian Central Bureau of Statistics.
2. Positive numbers imply a growth in the physical reserves of that resource during the year.
Source: Repetto *et al.*, 1989.

observed and used for valuation are the "correct" prices.

It is sometimes argued that physical accounts are of little or no use in establishing a link between environmental changes and economic effects, but this is not the case. For example, reasonably accurate relationships can be estimated between outputs of pollutants and the activities of industries and households using a combination of econometric approaches. In some cases, a physical input–output matrix may be constructed, so that the overall consequences of a change in the composition and level of final demand on several aspects of the environment can be calculated.

Hence physical accounts *are* useful in answering ecological questions of interest and in linking the environment to the economy. Recall that a fundamental feature of sustainable development is the recognition that environment and economy are necessarily interlinked. However, physical accounts are limited because they lack a common unit of measurement and it is not possible to gauge their importance relative to each other and to the non-environmental goods and services.

A review of the work to date on physical accounts in Norway indicates a mixed picture, with success in some areas and relative failure in others. The French environmental accounts which are also largely physical are very promising but a review of their usefulness in the policy and planning areas has yet to be made.

The monetary approaches that we have described are interesting and instructive but they have a number of difficulties. First, the question of what exactly we seek to measure is not totally resolved. If it is current welfare then a consumption adjusted measure is appropriate but if it is long-term welfare then some adjusted measure of GNP is required.

We recommend that a sustainable income concept be deployed. However, the adjustment that should be made to achieve this is still a matter of some debate. It is useful to think in terms of sustainable income, and some adjustments to gross-income measures that would achieve that have been described. But the suitability of sustainable income as a measure of long-term welfare is still unclear. We recommend further work in this area.

In practice the distinction between physical and monetary accounts need not be so clear-cut and it may be possible for some countries to establish both a physical stock-flow accounting system *and* a monetary income-expenditure statement.

In a sequence of workshops UNEP, the World Bank and UNSO have debated these questions and have reached a number of useful conclusions. We agree with these conclusions. The first is that, *at this stage*, the environmental accounts should not be fully incorporated into the national income accounts, but rather that a set of *satellite accounts* be established that deal with the environmental issues. Such accounts could be in physical or monetary terms or both and would seek to address the questions of the linkages between the environmental and natural resource base and the economic system, as well as estimating a natural resource balance sheet and working towards a measure of sustainable income.

However, the attainment of these goals is still some way off and the necessary work is only in its infancy.

The treatment of environmental accounts in the United Kingdom

In the United Kingdom no formal physical environmental accounting system exists but a number of relevant statistics are presented in the *Digest of Environmental Protection and Water Statistics*, published annually by the Department of the Environment. This document already contains a lot of useful information on physical measures of environmental pollution and environmental quality. This information has been assembled quite effectively without referring to, or using the frame-work of, physical resource accounting. Where it could possibly be developed further, however, is in the *linkage* between the physical environmental pollution and quality measures, and variables measuring the levels of economic activity in the different sectors of the economy. This would render the accounts more useful in quantifying the economy-environment relationships at various levels, a task which is critical to further work in this area.

On the monetary side, the United Kingdom has made no real effort to deal with the issues of valuing changes in the natural resource base that were discussed above. Oil, natural gas, coal, forest resources and fisheries are the main commodities that would need to be included and an appropriate procedure for valuing the stocks as well as the depreciation and growth would have to be established.

Conclusions and recommendations

From this review of environmental accounting the following conclusions emerge:

(i) the physical accounting option has been tried in a number of countries and is likely to be developed in a number of others. It can be useful in analysing the linkages between the environment and the economy and in forecasting future levels of demand on the natural and environmental resource base. However, its success in achieving these goals has been mixed, with some accounts being more useful than others;

(ii) the monetary accounting option has only been pursued partially. On the one hand work in Japan has produced a current welfare measure that takes account of some of the welfare consequences of environmental damage. Some effort is being made to develop a measure of net national income that is based on the notion of sustainability. Both these yield interesting results but are only part of the story;

(iii) the relationship between sustainable income and long-run welfare has not been fully established. However, there are strong reasons for supporting the measurement of sustainable income as the best proxy for long-run welfare.

In view of these conclusions, what options should the UK follow in the next few years? It could attempt to develop a system of national accounts along the lines of the French or the Norwegians. However, our view is that this is unlikely to be the best use of resources in this area. The cost of such an undertaking is likely to be very large and, as we have indicated, the returns are still unclear. On the other hand, some of the objectives of such an accounting system can be achieved by expanding the existing environmental database, *and developing the linkages between the environmental data and the economic demands on a piecemeal basis*. We would therefore recommend that these be looked at in greater detail.

As far as the monetary side of the accounts is concerned, there is a good case to be made for the measurement of sustainable income for the UK. This should incorporate measures of welfare loss due to environmental pollution as well as measures of depreciation in the natural and environmental resource base. The resources required for this task are probably less than those need for a full physical accounting framework, and the rewards somewhat clearer.

It should be noted while this exercise is being carried out that some benefit could be derived from similar projects being undertaken in other countries and could provide the impetus for measurement of sustainable income by the UN.

References

Corniere, P. (1986), "Natural resource (1) accounts in France. An example: inland waters", in *Information and Natural Resources* (Paris: OECD).

Devarajan, S., and R. J. Weiner (1988), "Natural resource depletion and national income accounts", mimeo. J. F. Kennedy School of Government, Harvard University.

Friend, A. (1988), "Natural resource accounting: a Canadian perspective", in Y. J. Ahmad, S. El Serafy and E. Lutz (eds), *Environmental and Resource Accounting and their Relevance to the Measurement of Sustainable Development* (Washington, DC: World Bank).

Hicks, J. A. (1946), *Value and Capital*, 2nd ed., (Oxford: Oxford University Press).

Mirrlees, J. A. (1969), "The evaluation of national income in an imperfect economy", *Pakistan Development Review*, Vol.9.

Nordhaus, W. D., and J. Tobin (1972), "Is growth obsolete?", *National Bureau of Economic Research*, General Series 96 (New York and London: Columbia University Press).

OECD (1988), "Natural resource accounting: the Norwegian experience". Prepared by A. Lone, Environment Committee, Group on the State of the Environment, Paris.

Repetto, R., W. Magrath, M. Wells, C. Beer, and F. Rossini, (1989), "Wasting assets: natural resource in the national income accounts" (Washington, DC: World Resources Institute).

United Nations (1968), "A system of national accounts", Statistical Methods, Series F, No. 3, United Nations, New York.

United Nations (1977), "Provisional international guidelines on the national and sectoral balance-sheet and reconciliation accounts of the system of national accounts", Statistical Papers, Series M, No. 60, Department of Social Affairs, New York.

United Nations (1980), "Future directions of work on the system of national accounts", Economic and Social Council, Statistical Commission, New York.

Uno, K. (1988), "Economic growth and environmental change in Japan – net national welfare and beyond", mimeo, Institute of Socio-economic Plannng, University of Tsukuba, Japan.

Weitzman, M. (1976), "On the welfare significance of national product in a dynamic economy", *Quarterly Journal of Economics*, 91.

5. PROJECT APPRAISAL

Project appraisal relates to the assessment of a capital investment, say building a road or airport, afforesting an area of land, building or renewing sea defences and so on. A *programme* is a set of projects. Projects in the *public sector* should, self-evidently, be assessed according to the goals and objectives of society as a whole which government represents. Projects in the *private sector* will be evaluated from the shareholder's perspective, i.e. they will tend to reflect the goals and objectives of the corporation on behalf of shareholders.

This difference raises the possibility that private sector decisions will be incompatible with society's broader goals, that "private and social profit" will diverge. Environmental quality is obviously one thing that might be neglected if corporations pursue profit motives alone. In practice, the corporate sector is increasingly taking environmental concerns into their planning (Box 5.1).

The way in which society ensures that the remaining potential for social and private profit divergence is minimized is through some form of *regulation*. The extent to which regulation *should* occur is of course a matter of political debate, but there are economic arguments which strongly bear on the issue.

In Chapter 7 we draw attention to ways in which the *cost of regulation* might be minimized by adopting a market-based approach to incentives for environmental improvement.

In this chapter we look at public-sector project appraisal.

The basic analytics of project appraisal

Project appraisal involves a comparison of costs and benefits.

Box 5.1 **The corporate response to environmental concerns**

ECONOMICS OF SUSTAINABLE DEVELOPMENT

An important issue for business? There are at least three reasons for thinking so:

- There are many signs that society has understated and undervalued the damage that has been done to natural and built environments. The economist's explanation is that many environmental costs are incurred 'external' to or outside the normal cash-flow streams of consumers, governments and enterprises. This can be seen in the context of pollution of rivers, seas and the atmosphere and loss of biological diversity.

- Second, consumer concern has risen in many countries. Some goods already display logos indicating they are environmentally benign. Green issues receive considerable media attention. A book on green consumerism was in the top ten best sellers for weeks running. The message is clear – there is a growing market in environmentally friendly products, even though the distinction between "environmentally-friendly" and other products is often not straightforward.

- Third, the modern environmental movement no longer argues for blanket preservation of all that is ecologically valuable. It speaks of the sustainable management of resources, of using resources while at the same time conserving them. Sustainable development is not just altering the way in which we look at the environment, but also opening up new opportunities for business, sometimes in partnership with conservationists.

Sustainable development calls for us to look at natural resources in the same way as we would look at a viable business; to get the optimum profit, or yield, whilst keeping the business assets intact or expanding. Environmentally sustainable development is just the same: getting as much as we can from our natural resources, the sustainable yield, without undermining the resource base.

If the 1970s' debate was about environment versus economic growth, will the 1990s' debate be about growth and development, where development is seen as improvement in our quality of life worldwide?

Source: International Chamber of Commerce, *Sustainable Development – the Business Approach* (Paris, 1989).

If benefits exceed costs, the project is, in principle, acceptable. Otherwise it is not. The exact rules that might be used to *rank* projects are discussed extensively in the literature. The basic formula for accepting a project is then:

$$\sum_{t=0}^{t=T} \{ B_t - C_t - E_t \} (1 + r)^{-t} > 0$$

where B_t is the benefit in time t
C_t is the cost in time t
E_t is the environmental damage done by the project (if there is an environmental improvement then $- E$ is replaced by $+ E$)
r is the *discount rate*.

Chapter 6 discusses the discount rate issue at length. In this basic project appraisal formula we have separated out non-environmental costs (C) and environmental costs (E) for purposes of illustrating two important ways of reflecting sustainable development considerations in project appraisal.

Valuing environmental damage

The discussion in Chapters 1 and 2 indicated a very important feature of sustainable development, namely *the necessity to ensure that environmental values are integrated into economic decision-making.* Chapter 7 shows how this might be done for the allocation of resources in general, i.e. through the price mechanism. As far as public project appraisal is concerned the implication is very straightforward: considerable effort is needed to ensure that the component E in the basic equation is evaluated. Various techniques for obtaining such valuations were outlined in Chapter 3.

This is not a novel conclusion. It has been the basis of the development of cost-benefit analysis techniques since the early 1960s. It is now widely accepted and, indeed, there is evidence now that environmental damage and environmental benefit estimation are increasingly being integrated into public sector decision-making.[1] The issue is the extent to which valuation procedures are actually employed and what the added potential is for their use.

Box 5.2   The costs and benefits of cost-benefit analysis in the USA

Among the many ways that benefit-cost analyses have influenced the development of regulations at EPA are the following:
(i)   Guiding the regulation's development,
(ii) Adding new alternatives,
(iii) Eliminating non-cost-effective alternatives,
(iv) Adjusting alternatives to account for differences between industries and segments,
(v)   Supporting decisions.
At times benefit-cost analysis has led to more efficient regulations by showing how more stringent alternatives would bring about a greater reduction in pollution without a commensurate increase in costs. In two instances (lead in fuels and small quantity generators) this led to the adoption of regulations that were more stringent than originally contemplated. At other times the analysis showed that the costs of more stringent regulations would be disproportional to the expected benefits. In three instances (used oil, TSCA premanufacture review, FIFRA data requirements) this led to the selection of less stringent regulatory alternatives that resulted in reduced regulatory burdens without significant reductions in environmental improvement.

While these improvements cannot be attributed solely to benefit-cost analysis, it is fair to say that the analyses played major roles in bringing about the regulatory improvements. The most dramatic potential increases in the estimated net benefits from regulation are summarized as follows:

EIA	*Change in regulation*	*Potential increase in total net benefits of regulations*
Lead in fuels	more stringent standard, greater health and welfare benefits	$6.7 billion
Used oil	reduced regulatory costs, greater reduction in risk	$3.6 billion
Premanufacture review	reduced regulatory costs, no significant reduction in effectiveness	$40 million

The contributions of the benefit-cost analyses prepared by EPA go beyond individual regulations, however. In addition to improving individual environmental regulations, benefit-cost analyses also have increased awareness of the environmental results of EPA's regulations, provided a framework for comparing regulations both within a single medium and across media, identified cross-media effects, and improved analytic techniques.

Source: United States Environmental Protection Agency, *EPA's Use of Benefit-Cost Analysis*, US EPA, Washington DC, August 1987.

The *cost-effectiveness* of such environmental valuation procedures is richly illustrated by experience in the United States.
Box 5.2 illustrates the kinds of gains that the United States
Environmental Protection Agency assesses have been made by
adopting cost-benefit procedures in their choice of regulatory
options for environmental control.

How might the United Kingdom further its use of environmental valuation?

Guidance is provided by the Treasury to government departments on how to appraise investments through a "Green Book-
let" (UK Treasury, 1984). In general, the guidance is to adopt
discounted cash-flow approaches. In respect of "intangible" costs
and benefits the Treasury advises:

> Many costs and benefits are measured directly in money terms: for
> example savings in expenditure on resources, and sales revenues.
> Where they are not (examples are travel time saved, noise and
> other forms of pollution, and broad managerial or political factors)
> costs and benefits can sometimes still sensibly be given money
> values, often by analyzing people's actual behaviour and declared
> or revealed preferences. These imputed money values can be used
> in the appraisal as if they were actual cash flows. Other factors
> which cannot be valued should be listed, and quantified as far as
> practicable, making it clear that they are additional factors to be
> taken into account. It can sometimes be helpful to calculate the
> value which such factors would have to take for the net present
> value of a scheme to turn positive or negative . . . .
>
> Account sometimes needs to be taken of the value which
> individuals may place now on the possibility of using a service or
> visiting an attractive area even when they do not currently use the
> service or make visits. (UK Treasury, 1984, paras 33 and 34)[2]

Interestingly, these brief statements imply quite an extensive
acknowledgement of benefit estimation principles. The reference to actual behaviour and declared and revealed preferences
makes it clear that both surrogate markets (e.g. hedonic prices
from property markets) and hypothetical markets (contingent
valuation) could qualify. The use of "what if" valuations – i.e.
finding what the value would be for a net present value (NPV) to

become positive or negative – is widely used in actual cost-benefit studies. The "what if" value is then compared to some intuitive appraisal of what the benefits might be. Finally, the last sentence quite explicitly encompasses the concept of option value (but not existence value).

It is also now clear that the UK Treasury is embracing more damage and benefit estimation techniques than hitherto.[3] But it would now be advisable for the Treasury to update its guidelines with more explicit advice on ways in which monetary valuation techniques can be used to assist project appraisal. While the focus should be on using both fairly sophisticated monetary valuation techniques, it is also possible that some basic rules of thumb might be developed whereby minimum "unit values" are established.

Further impetus to applying valuation techniques more extensively may come from the European Community Directive on Environmental Impact Assessment (EIA). In July 1988, the UK formally complied with the Directive. Under the Directive certain projects, listed in the Annex of that report, must be subject to an EIA.[4] Assessment must relate to impacts on humans, flora and fauna; soil, water, air and climate; and material assets and cultural heritage. The EEC Directive does not require any form of benefits or damage assessment in the sense of monetary evaluations. In principle, however, such assessments would probably fit the overall requirements for the type of information that a developer must supply. These include, for example, "a description of the likely significant effects on the environment".

Other UK Ministries do have their own appraisal manuals. In no case, however, do they encompass guidance on the monetary evaluation of environmental impacts. Monetary evaluation is, of course, not the only way of securing a "proper" role for environmental dimensions in project planning. Environmental Impact Assessment (EIA) seeks to do this and there are other means of reflecting environmental values in decision-making.

The UK Overseas Development Administration (ODA) has several relevant documents on project appraisal. A "user friendly" approach to project planning in general is given in its 1983 guide *Planning Development Projects*.[5] However this contains nothing on environmental issues. A 1988 guide has sections on environmental evaluation which are taken from a publication originally produced for the Asian Development Bank.[6] ODA has also issued a *Manual of Environmental Appraisal* but this does not address the issue of valuing environmental impacts.[7] It seems fair to say therefore that current ODA procedures do not directly address the issue of how to evaluate environmental impacts in terms of either monetary valuation or some "importance indicators". The ODA work does, however, directly address the issues of integrating environmental concerns into project appraisal. The valuation issue is now being addressed in an additional guidelines/manual document due in 1990.[8]

The UK Department of Transport has a computerized approach to investment appraisal.[9] This enables a standard programme to be adapted to local conditions in terms of the relevant parameters, e.g. traffic flows, so that benefits or costs are produced for time values, operating costs and accidents. These benefits and/or costs are then fed into a comparison with the construction and running costs of the road. Accident valuations are based on a standard "value of life", currently £500,000,[10] and a standard value for non-fatal injuries. The Department of Transport's approach to environmental valuation is interesting. Monetary evaluation is explicitly rejected but environmental impacts are carefully listed and measured. This reflects the original advice of the Advisory Committee on Trunk Road Assessment[11] to the effect that monetary evaluation was infeasible but that environmental impacts clearly mattered. The Standing Environmental Committee on Trunk Road Assessment (SATRA) has apparently considered the evidence on monetary evaluation on a number of occasions since. It is not clear how this sceptical approach to monetary evaluation relates to the experience with monetary evaluation elsewhere.

An additional approach to project appraisal: integrating sustainability into cost-benefit analysis

The prime requirement for project appraisal improvement is the integration of environmental values into cost-benefit analysis (CBA). Chapter 6 will argue that adjustments should typically *not* be made to the underlying "real" discount rate in project appraisal. That is, the discount rate should be determined by conventional considerations (discussed in Chapter 6). However, this conclusion is contingent upon the proper evaluation of environmental gains and losses in project appraisal. This "raising of the profile" of environmental effects can be further strengthened in the following way.

Sustainability can be introduced into CBA by setting a constraint on the depletion and degradation of the stock of natural capital. Essentially, the economic efficiency objective is modified to mean that all projects yielding net benefits should be undertaken subject to the requirement that environmental damage (i.e. natural capital depreciation) should be zero or negative. However, applied at the level of *each project* such a requirement would be stultifying. Few projects would be feasible. At the *programme* level, however, the interpretation is more interesting. It amounts to saying that, netted out across a set of projects (programme), the *sum* of individual damages should be zero or negative. That is, if E_i is the *damage* done by the ith project, we require that:

$$\sum_i E_i \leq 0$$

Such a formulation ignores time. It is possible to show that two formulations of the sustainability constraint emerge.[12] Under *weak sustainability* it is the present value of E_i, $PV(E_i)$, which is constrained to be non-positive. Under *strong sustainability* each E_i is constrained to be non-positive *for each period* of time.

Since it is not feasible to set $PV(E_i)$ to be zero or negative for each project, but it is feasible to set $\sum_i E_i$ to be non-positive, the sustainability constraint amounts to including within any portfolio of investments one or more *shadow projects,* the aim of which is to compensate for the environmental damage from the other projects in the portfolio. The conventional CBA rule would then apply to the *environmentally depleting* projects, i.e.

$$\sum_t d^t . \sum_i (B_{it} - C_{it} - E_{it}) > 0.$$

(where B is non-environmental benefits, C is non-environmental costs, E is net environmental costs or benefits, t is time, and d^t is the discount factor).

The *environmentally compensating* project(s), j, would be chosen such that

$$\sum_j PV(A_j) = \sum_i PV(E_i)$$

for the weak sustainability criterion and

$$\sum_j A_{jt} = \sum_i E_{it} \qquad \text{for all t}$$

for the strong sustainability criterion, where the jth project is designed to compensate for the damage done by the other projects. For the compensating projects, then, the normal CBA decision rule does not apply, although we would wish to minimize the cost of achieving the sustainability criterion.

An alternative approach to adopting environmentally compensating projects is widely suggested, namely lowering the discount rate for environmentally beneficial projects relative to those that generate environmental damage. It is possible to show that adjusting discount rates for some "environmental risk premium" can produce similar results to those suggested here, but the adjustments are complex and actually determining the risk premium for damaging projects (or the discount for beneficial projects) is liable to generate impossible informational demands.

Yet another suggestion, that *all* projects should attract a lower discount rate, can actually be counterproductive of the basic idea of maintaining natural capital stocks. This is because lower discount rates encourage a larger *total* of investment and this will drag through the system more materials and energy and hence more waste (see Chapter 6). We conclude that the "compensating project" idea has the potential for modifying project appraisal so as better to represent the sustainable development ideal.

In practice what a sustainability constraint would mean is:

(i) checking carefully what environmental impacts a given *programme* of investments is likely to have;
(ii) adjusting the programme in such a way that the overall net damage is as close to zero as is possible;
(iii) adopting as the means of adjusting the portfolio of investments particular projects which generate environmental benefits.

For agencies with wide-ranging portfolios such adjustments of programmes would mean more spent on environment and less on projects with negative environmental impacts. While that may seem contrary to the spirit of "development" we need to recall that this change in the *balance* of development is exactly what sustainable development calls for. For agencies which might appear to be engaged in activities that appear to be systematically environmentally destructive (road building for example) the focus will be on minimising that environmental damage, quantifying the damage where it is likely to occur and ensuring that this affects the decisions on both the amount and design of roads, and quantifying environmental *benefits* when they occur (e.g. reduced noise and improved urban amenity from bypasses). At the level of central allocation of funds, the sustainability principle means shifting the balance of funding of agencies in favour of those that generate positive environmental benefits and against those generating negative environmental impacts.

Conclusions

Sustainable development has two implications for project appraisal arising from the emphasis in sustainable development on *value* and a *longer-term* view. The first implication is that,

• efforts to integrate environmental values into project appraisal should be greatly extended, both at the level of understanding environmental effects and at the level of valuing those effects.

The second implication requires more research, but it involves the idea of

• making *programmes* of investment subject to a sustainability constraint to the effect that, as far as possible, environmental capital in the aggregate is not reduced.

Notes

1. For a survey of benefit estimation procedures and uses in six countries – UK, USA, Italy, Germany, Norway and Netherlands – see D. W. Pearce, *Benefits Estimates and Environmental Decision-Making* (Paris: OECD, 1989).
2. UK Treasury, *Investment Appraisal in the Public Sector: A Technical Guide for Government Departments* (London: HM Treasury, 1984).
3. For a survey of benefit estimation studies in the United Kingdom see Anil Markandya, David Pearce and R. Kerry Turner, *The Use of Environmental Benefits Estimates in Decision-Making: the Case of the United Kingdom* (Paris: Environment Directorate, OECD, 1989).
4. In brief, these are oil refineries, large power stations, radioactive waste storage facilities, iron and steel works, asbestos extracting/processing, chemical installations, roads, railway lines, airports, ports and inland waterways and hazardous waste installations.
5. G. A. Bridger and J. Winpenny, *Planning Development Projects* (London: Overseas Development Administration, 1983).
6. J. MacArthur, *Appraisal of Projects in Developing Countries: a Guide for Economists* (London: Overseas Development Administration, 1988, third version). The material on environment is taken from J. Dixon *et al.*, *Economic Analysis of the Environmental Impacts of Development Projects*, (Manila: Asian Development Bank, 1986). This latter publication has since been revised and updated as J. Dixon *et al.*, *Economic Analysis of the Environmental Impacts of Development*

Projects (London: Earthscan Publications, 1988).

7. ODA, *Manual of Environmental Appraisal* (London: ODA, 1989).

8. J. Winpenny, *Guide to Economic Evaluation of Environmental Effects* (provisional title, in process).

9. The programme and the accompanying manual is known as COBA and is currently in its ninth version.

10. This is an increase from the previous sum of £252,000 and reflects a review of the procedures in 1988 which concluded that values should be based on willingness to pay measures. DTp is currently reviewing the valuation of non-fatal injuries which are currently based on a "cost of illness" rather than willingness to pay approach.

11. Advisory Committee on Trunk Road Assessment, *Report* (the "Leitch Committee") (London: HMSO, 1977).

12. See D. W. Pearce, E. Barbier, A. Markandya, *Sustainable Development and Cost-Benefit Analysis* (London Environmental Economics Centre, 1988).

6. DISCOUNTING THE FUTURE

The nature of discounting

Chapter 1 explained that economic analysis tends to proceed on the basis that "economic value" reflects people's preferences. Those preferences exhibit themselves in market and non-market situations, and there is no rational basis for designing economic policy as if only *some* preferences mattered, i.e. those expressed in the market place.

But individuals also express preferences about *when* benefits and costs are desired. Typically, the later a cost or benefit occurs, the less it matters. The implicit weighting of the present over the future is known as *discounting* and the rate at which the weight changes is the *discount rate*. Simple rationales for discounting are as follows.

Suppose that you are offered £1 now or you can wait for that £1 until next year. Assume for the moment that you are certain to be alive next year and the availability of the £1 next year is guaranteed. Will you wait or will you prefer to have the £1 now? Since the sum is the same, any preference exhibited for taking the money now is an instance of discounting. Typically, people will take the money now. Why? There are several reasons.

(i) With the £1, capital can be purchased, which can then be put to productive use. The existence of such productive opportunities means that in a year's time the capital plus what it has generated will be worth more than £1, say £1.10. Effectively, then the choice becomes one of accepting £1 now or £1.10 next year. In the economist's language, there is positive *capital productivity*. So, the first reason for discounting is *capital productivity*.

(ii) Even if capital investment was not productive in the sense outlined above people would still probably prefer the £1 now rather than next year. This is because people are *impatient*, or, to use the economist's language, they have *time preference*. As long as we honour the requirement to respect people's preferences, time preference also becomes a reason for discounting.

The simple arithmetic of discounting is illustrated in Box 6.1.

Box 6.1   **The arithmetic of discounting**

Suppose that the "real" (i.e. net of inflation) rate of interest is 7 per cent. Then the value of £1 today is treated as being equal to the amount you would need to invest today to receive £1 in one year's time, in two years' time and so on.

At 7 per cent interest one would need to invest £1/1.07 = 0.935 to obtain £1 in one year's time. Hence the discount factor for one year is 0.935.

Similarly to obtain £1 in two years' time one would need to invest £1/$(1.07)^2$ now. This equals 0.873, which is the discount factor two years hence.

After 10 years the discount factor becomes $1/(1.07)^{10} = 0.508$, and after 50 years it becomes $1/(1.07)^{50}$ years = 0.034.

The higher the interest rate, the smaller the discount factor becomes, and the faster it falls with time.

There are additional reasons for discounting.

(iii) If we relax the assumption that the individual can be certain to be alive and well to receive the £1 next year, his or her preference for the £1 now becomes stronger. This is the *risk of death* argument for discounting and might be subsumed under the "impatience" argument in that we now have "pure impatience" ("pure myopia" as it is termed in the literature) and "risk of death impatience".

(iv) We cannot be certain that the £1 will be there next year.

Anything might happen to prevent it being available. This is the *risk and uncertainty* argument for discounting. Again, we can add it in to our general argument about impatience favouring the present over the future.

(v) If in the future we, or our descendants, can confidently expect to be better off than we are now, it would be reasonable to argue that £1 would be worth less to them that it is to us. That is, less "value" (or "utility") will be attached to the £1 twenty years hence. This is the *diminishing marginal utility* argument for discounting.

We can bring all the arguments together by saying that there are two basic reasons for discounting:

(i) the *social time preference* rationale says that people simply prefer the present to the future because of pure impatience, risk of death, uncertainty about the future and diminishing (marginal) utility of consumption. This is the social time preference rate of discount (STPR).

(ii) the *social cost of capital* argument says that we should discount the future at the rate of return achievable on the last unit of capital investment in the economy. This is the social opportunity cost rate of discount (SOC).

However, the two ways of deriving discount rates do not, in general, produce the same result. Hence we tend to have to choose one rate or the other. Alternatively, we can seek to combine the rates in some way: that is the topic of a substantial literature.[1]

In the United Kingdom the rate set by the Treasury for use in cost-benefit and project appraisal generally is 5 per cent in real terms, and sometimes a rate of 7 per cent. Exceptions are made for afforestation which has a "special rate" of 3 per cent for reasons we investigate below. The 5 per cent is broadly meant to reflect the rate of return on new investment in the private sector. The basic rationale is thus a SOC one. It says that investment in the public sector should achieve at least 5 per cent because otherwise the money invested would have secured a 5 per cent or higher rate of return in the private sector. Public sector investments securing less than 5 per cent would therefore be using resources inefficiently.[2]

Resource allocation decisions should be made on the basis of *social returns*. The social rate of return to an investment can differ from the rate of return to the private investor or resource owner because of the unpriced impacts the investment might have. The rate of return to a new coal-fired power station, for example, ought to include deductions for damage done by pollution emissions. The same logic applies to the choice of discount rate. Strictly, the *social* opportunity cost of capital is what matters if the SOC argument is used for selecting discount rates. In the remainder of this chapter we evaluate various arguments for adjusting the "market" interest rate to accommodate environmental concerns. If the arguments are valid, and a downward adjustment is warranted, in some or all cases, this could have significant implications for the projects that would be selected within the public sector. Hence the question being examined is one of great potential importance.

Discounting and the environment

From an environmental standpoint the choice of a discount rate works in differing directions. With a high discount rate, fewer investments are undertaken, particularly investments with long-term payoffs and large initial costs. These include investments such as water management projects, including hydroelectric projects. This means that the preservation of certain natural areas is more likely to be achieved at higher discount rates. On the other hand, higher discount rates imply a more rapid development of exhaustible resources and shorter rotation periods and smaller stocks of renewable resources. For exhaustible resources this leads to the conservationists' fear that stocks will be depleted faster than substitute fuels can be made available at reasonable prices.

For renewable resources, the implications of smaller stocks for environmental preservation are obvious. In addition, investment projects in forestry are unlikely to be justifiable, because of the long gestation periods involved in the investments (particularly slow-growing species).

In addition to the considerations discussed above, environmental factors can be directly affected by the choice of the discount rate. One major impact that arises is that projects with *potentially catastrophic consequences* do not get a fair "hearing" with positive discounting.

For example, suppose that a particular programme involves a significant probability of a major catastrophe through soil contamination in a hundred years' time. The cost of this contamination is estimated, in today's prices, to be £100 million and the probability that it would occur is 0.5. Then the expected cost in 2089 is £50 million. Discounted at 10 per cent per annum this amounts to £3629, at 5 per cent it amounts to £380 227 and at 2 per cent it amounts to £6 901 653. Although the discount rate makes a considerable difference to the discounted present value of the cost, *none* of these figures is likely to sway the decision on the justification of the project. Hence there is a genuine concern that, with discounting, catastrophic future costs are not given their true importance. Box 6.2 illustrates this further.

The environmentalist critique of discounting

In the light of some of the effects of discounting, environmentalists have urged a requestioning of the fundamental arguments for discounting. In fact, however, there is no unique relationship between high discount rates and environmental deterioration as is often supposed. Thus, high rates may well shift cost burdens forward to later generations, but, if the discount rate is allowed to determine the level of investment, they will also slow down the general pace of development through the depressing effect on investment. Since natural resources are required for investment, the *demand* for natural resources is generally less with high discount rates than with low ones. High rates will also discourage development projects that compete with existing environmentally benign land uses – e.g. watershed development as opposed to an existing wilderness use. Exactly how the choice of discount rate impacts on the *overall* profile of natural

Box 6.2   **The "tyranny" of discounting**

Concern about the effects of discounting arises for two main reasons: it appears to shift the burden of costs to future generations, and it precludes future generations from inheriting created natural wealth.

The burden-shifting was illustrated in the text. A radiation hazard 100 years from now due to, say, stored waste and costing £1 billion in environmental and health damage would have the following present value (assuming a 5 per cent discount rate):

$$£ \frac{1,000,000,000}{(1.05)^{50}} = £87.2 \text{ million}$$

The £1 billion has been reduced to one-tenth its cost at the time of occurrence. Notice, however, that if the discount rate is roughly equal to the prevailing interest rate, the £87.2 million could be set aside now to accumulate at 5 per cent so as to provide a fund for compensating future generations for the damage. This is why some experts argue for the *actual* compensation of the future, i.e. the creation of compensation funds. In the example given, the fund would be difficult to determine since the *occurrence* of the event is uncertain (i.e. its probability may not be known), its *scale* is uncertain, and its *timing* is uncertain (and this affects the size of the principal sum to be set aside). Some fund may of course be better than none at all, but the complexity of "intergenerational compensation" is illustrated by the example.

Note that where timing, scale and probability are known, such funds make good sense. An example would be the decommissioning of a nuclear power station. Its "life" is known, the probability of decommissioning is one, and costs are now known with more certainty.

The other area of concern is the effect of discounting on the inheritance of the future. The conspicuous example is forestry, but the analysis holds for any renewable resource with a long "gestation" period. In this case the benefit of a tree that takes 50 years to grow appears to be reduced to comparative insignificance in terms of present values. The result is that unless special treatment is afforded to afforestation (as it is in the UK) the trees will not be grown and the future will have "forgone" a benefit which they cannot reproduce (because they will have to wait 50 years too).

But even here the "tyranny of discounting" must not be exaggerated. Much of the criticism of discounting really arises because the critics feel that the tree, in this case, is being *undervalued*. This is why we stress the importance of valuation in the text. But proper valuation is not sufficient for the idea of passing on inherited natural wealth would ensure more afforestation, not less (leaving aside the debate about the *type* of afforestation).

resource and environment use in any country is thus ambiguous. This point is important since it reduces considerably the force of arguments to the effect that conventionally determined discount rates should be lowered (or raised, depending on the view taken) to accommodate environmental considerations.

None the less, it is the case that concern for the environmental dimension of development policy has led to a questioning of the basic rationale for discounting. We outline below some of the points that have been raised. *Note that what is being argued generally is that if we cannot substantiate the case for positive discounting, the presumption must be that a zero discount rate is, initially anyway, the more appropriate choice.*

We consider the objections to the arguments for discounting under four headings and take each in turn.

1. Pure time preference
The objections to permitting pure time preference to influence social discount rates are as follows. First, individual time preference is not necessarily consistent with individual lifetime welfare maximization. The proof is complex and is not discussed here. This is a variant of the more general view that time discounting, because of impatience, is generally irrational. Second, what individuals want carries no necessary implications for public policy. This amounts, of course, to a rejection of the underlying value judgement of cost-benefit comparisons, namely that individual preferences matter. Third, the underlying value judgement is improperly expressed. A society that elevates want-satisfaction to high status should recognize that it is the satisfaction of wants *as they arise* that matters. But this means that tomorrow's satisfaction matters, not today's assessment of tomorrow's satisfaction. Fourth, if the "risk of death" argument is used, it is illegitimate to derive implications for potentially immortal societies from risks faced by mortal individuals.

What view is taken on the normative relevance of pure time preference depends on the acceptability of one or more of these objections. We would argue that to overturn the basic value judgement underlying the cost-benefit style appraisal requires good reason: i.e. the rationale for paternalism should be a strong one. We would surmise that such arguments may exist in some countries, but would not be generally acceptable in the UK. Philosophically, the argument that the value judgement needs re-expressing in line with the third observation above is impressive. However, its practical relevance to the determination of interest rates remains unclear.

2. Risk and uncertainty

It has been argued that a benefit or cost is valued less the more uncertain is its occurrence. Since uncertainty is usually expected to increase with time from the present, this declining value becomes a function of time and hence is formally expressed in the form of a discount rate for risk and uncertainty.

The types of uncertainty that are generally regarded as being of relevance (although they are very often confused) are:

(i) uncertainty about the presence of the individual at some future date (the "risk of death" argument),
(ii) uncertainty about the preferences of the individual even when his existence can be regarded as certain,
(iii) uncertainty about the availability of the benefit or the existence of the cost.

The objections to using uncertainty to justify positive discount rates are several.

First, uncertainty arising from not being sure that the individual will be present to receive a distant benefit – the "risk of death" argument – ignores the argument presented earlier about the "immortality" of society in contrast to the mortality of the individual. Indeed, a number of attempts have been made to measure time preference rates using survival probabilities.

Second, uncertainty about preferences is clearly relevant if we are talking about certain goods and perhaps even aspects of environmental conservation (as the "environmentalism" of the 1970s and 1980s demonstrates), but hardly seems relevant if we are considering projects or policies whose output is food, shelter, water and energy. If anything, we can be more sure of future preferences for these goods, not less.

Third, uncertainty about the presence or scale of benefits and costs may be unrelated to time, and certainly appears unlikely to be related in such a way that the scale of risk obeys an exponential function as is implied in the use of a single rate in the discount factor:

$$e^{-rt,} \text{ or } 1/(1+r)^t$$

What is being argued here is not that uncertainty and risk are irrelevant to the decision-guiding rule, but that their presence should not be handled by adjustments to the discount rate. For such adjustments imply a particular behaviour for the risk premium which it is hard to justify. This argument is in fact widely accepted by economists, although it appears to underlie the 2 per cent attached to the officially recommended 5 per cent "test discount rate" in the United Kingdom in the presence of "benefit optimism".

If uncertainty does not take on a form consistent with exponential increase, the suggestion is that risk and uncertainty are better handled by other means – i.e. via adjustments to cost and benefit streams, leaving the underlying discount rate unadjusted for risk. This argument seems to us to be correct. It is worth noting, however, that adding a premium to the discount rate for risk *is* widely recommended.

3. Diminishing marginal utility of consumption
Critics question the diminishing marginal utility component of STPR, suggesting either that it is irrelevant because it is not an observable or measurable entity, or that it could take any value, including negative ones, since the rate of growth of consumption could be greater or less than zero.

Many economists dispute whether there is any meaningful way of measuring the utility of consumption. This is a complex debate which we do not review here. Empirical estimates do exist.

What can we conclude on diminishing marginal utility? Its suitability as a source of discounting appears to be reasonably unambiguous only in contexts where we can reliably expect sustainable changes in real consumption per capita. In countries where environmental damage is high, those conditions may well not pertain. If high personal time preference rates are allowed to influence the value of STPR the implication may therefore be that the discount rate unjustly reflects constrained activity, a situation where individuals are unable to act in a normal economic and environmental framework. This raises questions about the validity of such rates, perhaps abandoning the search for a social time preference rate altogether, or modifying the choice rate to reflect the constraints on behaviour. The problem then is that there are no clear rules for choosing a discount rate.

4. Opportunity cost of capital

As observed previously, the position taken by many economists is that the "proper" social rate of discount is the rate of return on the marginal project displaced by investment in question.

It has to be recalled that the function of the discount rate is to assist in the process of allocating capital funds. This offers a *prima facie* bias in favour of rates reflecting returns on displaced investment.

The environmental literature has made some limited attempts to discredit discounting due to opportunity cost arguments. This literature is, however, confusing since most of the objections arise because the *implication* of opportunity cost discounting is that some rate greater than zero emerges and this is then held to be inconsistent with a concept of intergenerational justice. This aspect of the debate is considered shortly. There do, however, appear to be two criticisms which are generally, but not wholly, independent of this wider concern.

The first arises because the discount *factor* arising from a constant discount *rate* takes on a specific exponential form. This is because discounting is simply the reciprocal of compound interest. In turn, compound interest implies that if we invest £100 today it will compound forward to a particular rate, *provided* we keep not just the original £100 invested but also reinvest the profits. Now suppose the profits are consumed rather than reinvested. The critics suggest that this means that those consumption flows have no opportunity cost. What, they say, is the relevance of a discount rate based on assumed reinvested profits if in fact the profits are not reinvested but consumed?

If the argument is correct it provides a reason for not using a *particular* rate – the opportunity cost rate – for discounting streams of consumption flows as opposed to streams of profits which are always reinvested. But, in that context, it would not provide a reason for rejecting *discounting* altogether, since consumption flows should be discounted at a social time preference rate. That is, the critics have not seen that a future holiday *is* worth less than a current holiday if we admit any of the arguments for a social time preference rate. As it happens, the particular critics in question would not admit to believing the arguments for time preference rates either, so their position would be consistent.

The second argument relates to intertemporal compensation. Consider an investment which has an expected environmental damage of £X in some future time period T. Should this £X be discounted to a present value? The argument for doing so on opportunity cost grounds is presumably something like the following. If we debit the investment with a social cost *now* of $£X/(1+r)^T$, then that sum can be invested at r% now and it will grow to be £X in year T and can then be used to compensate the future sufferers of the environmental damage. Critics argue that this argument has confused two issues. The first is whether the future damage matters less than current damage of a similar scale. The second is whether we can devise schemes to compensate for future damage. The answer to the first question, they argue, is that it does not matter less than current damage, or if it does, it matters less only because we are *able* to compensate the future as shown. If we are not able to make the compensation, the argument for being less concerned, and hence the argument for discounting, become irrelevant.

Part of the problem here is that actual and "potential" compensation are being confused. As typically interpreted, cost-benefit rules require only that we could, hypothetically, compensate losers, not that we actually do. In this case, the resource cost to the current generation of hypothetically compensating a future generation is, quite correctly, the discounted value of the compensation. Really the objection is to the absence of built-in *actual* compensation mechanisms in cost-benefit appraisals. We have considerable sympathy with that view, but it is *not* relevant to the issue of how to choose a discount rate.

These particular arguments against opportunity cost related discounting are not, in our view, persuasive. It seems fair to say, however, that they are not regarded by their advocates as the most forceful that can be advanced against discount rates *per se*. Those rest with arguments about intergenerational justice and these are dealt with shortly.

Conclusions on "environmental critiques" of discounting

The environmental debate has undoubtedly contributed to intellectual soul-searching on the rationale for discounting. But, in our view, it has not been successful in demonstrating a case for rejecting discounting as such. It does raise issues of concern with respect to the use of rates of interest which reflect pure time preference, but it does not provide a case for rejecting pure time preference completely. It also raises further concerns about the compatibility of time-preference based discounting and opportunity cost discounting especially in the context of poor developing countries. We further observed that traditional arguments for securing "risk premia" on discount rates are fallacious: risk and uncertainty are properly handled in investment appraisal through adjustments to costs and benefits streams, not the discount rate. Lastly, we found environmental critiques of opportunity cost rates wanting, deferring consideration, however, of the wider intergenerational arguments.

The environmental critique that discount rates are in some sense "too high" reflects real concerns, but these concerns are better dealt with by *not* adjusting discount rates, but through other means that we describe shortly.

Discounting and natural resources

So far the discussion has been in terms of environmental effects in general, and their impact on discount rates. There are, however, one set of such effects that merit special consideration. These are the repercussions of the discount rate on the management of natural resources.

The choice of the discount rate has a particular effect on the rate of exploitation of natural resources. The basic decision with regard to such resources is how much to consume now and how much to hold in store for future consumption. It is intuitively clear that this decision is going to be influenced by the price of present versus future consumption – i.e. the discount rate. The higher the discount rate, the faster is the rate of depletion of the resource in the earlier years and the shorter is the interval before which the resource is exhausted. With a higher discount rate, a lower value is placed on future consumption relative to present consumption. Hence it is fairly clear that depletion policy, which seeks to maximize the discounted net benefits from a given stock of the resource, will prefer present consumption as the discount rate rises.

With renewable resources, the discount rate determines the rate of harvesting. The higher this rate is, the more intense is the harvesting effort and so the consumption of the resource requires a *sustainable* rate of use of resource. This means that in the long run the rate of harvesting must equal the rate of regeneration. However, it is possible, if the discount rate rises above the maximum biological growth rate of the stock, that, under certain conditions, the resources will be depleted and extinguished altogether.

High discount rates, which may be acceptable on other grounds, can therefore have undesirable consequences for projects involving natural resources. In spite of this, however, in our view the use of a lower discount rate is not the best policy to follow with regard to natural resources. To begin with, there is the question of which project should qualify. Inevitably there will be grey areas and this would cause further problems. Second, there are a number of situations in which private decisions are central to the resource exploitation problem, and discount rate changes for these groups are not a practicable or efficient policy. Third, even if one used lower discount rates, there is no guarantee that some serious resource degradation might not occur.

As a result of these considerations some additional concern is required which ensures that,

(i) *renewable* resources are managed *sustainably*, a familiar concept to foresters and fishermen, but not one that is always practised;

(ii) *exhaustible* resources are depleted in such a way that a significant proportion of the "rents" from them are reinvested in resources which will compensate for the exhaustible resource when it is depleted.

Should discount rates be adjusted because of environmental concern?

Much of the modern discussion on how to integrate environmental factors into investment appraisal has tried to do so by making adjustments to discount rates. The two main kinds of adjustments that have been sought are:

(i) adding a premium to discount rates to reflect risk and uncertainty about environmental consequences of investments;

(ii) lowering discount rates to reflect the interests of future generations.

We argue that neither argument constitutes a reason for adjusting discount rate. But because we will be arguing that these very relevant and important factors *do* need to be taken into account in the appraisal of investments and in general policy, we need to be sure that we understand why the arguments for making adjustments to the discount rate are not persuasive.

1. Environmental risk
It is not advisable to adjust discount rates to reflect *environmental risk*. Essentially this is because such an adjustment assumes risk to behave in a manner that is very unlikely to be realistic. We can consider an example. Consider an investment which

has a high environmental cost in the final years of the project, perhaps arising because of the need to dismantle equipment which contains toxic materials. Now assume that we are uncertain about the size of this cost. The uncertainty ought to make the investment less attractive compared to a situation in which we knew the dismantling costs with certainty. If we raise the discount rate this will certainly be the effect. However, while the *direction* of adjustment is correct, we have no foundation for believing that the present value of the dismantling cost has been accurately represented by the adjustment to the discount rate. In theory, it is possible under special circumstances to obtain a discount rate which reflects the risk. In practice, we argue that adjusting discount rates for risk is not an efficient procedure because it imposes a time-profile for risk on to the project which has no particular justification, and because it requires information on "certainty equivalence" (see below) that is more effectively used directly in the valuation of the project.

The problem of accommodating risk can be overcome by using *certainty equivalence* procedures. A simple example will suffice here. Box 6.3 gives a cost-benefit profile for an hypothetical project. The second column shows the expected net benefits. These are the *average* values arising from assessing the chances of the benefit occurring. For example, if the net benefit in year two is a 50 per cent chance of £200 and a 50 per cent chance of nothing, the expected value is £100 (0.5 × 200) + (0.5 × 0). The third column contains the adjustment to risk (sometimes confusingly termed the "risk discount factor"). What this adjustment shows is the way in which attitudes to risk modify the expected values. Thus in year 2 the expected net benefit is 100. This might be compared to a return of 90 that is expected with complete certainty. That is, we would be indifferent between the "gamble" of the 100 and an absolutely certain return of 90. This adjustment converts the expected net benefits to their *certainty equivalents*. For example, the expected value of £100 in year two is risky. We are likely to prefer a smaller but certain sum of money to this risky £100. This smaller sum is shown as £90 in column 4 and hence 0.1 is the risk adjustment. *Notice that in this example the risk adjustment has nothing to do with time.*

Box 6.3   **Risk adjustment and discounting: an example**

Year	Expected net benefit	Risk adjustment	Certainty equivalent	Discount factor	Adjusted flows
1	−100.0	1.0	−100.0	1.0	−100.0
2	+100.0	0.9	+ 90.0	0.95	+ 85.5
3	+100.0	0.8	+ 80.0	0.91	+ 72.8
4	+100.0	0.75	+ 75.0	0.86	+ 64.5
5	− 80.0	1.20	− 96.0	0.82	− 78.7
					+ 44.1

This should be sufficient to differentiate adjustments for risk from adjustments for time discounting. This is shown in column 5 using a hypothetical 5 per cent discount rate.

2. Irreversibility
One special environmental consideration that might, *prima facie*, imply the adjustment of the discount rate is that of irreversibility. The issue, as the term implies, is that the costs associated with a large number of decisions are *irreversible*. A valley that is flooded for a hydroelectric dam cannot be restored to its original state. Ancient buildings that are pulled down for a road development may be reproducible if dismantled and moved, but usually are lost for ever. Radioactive waste, once produced, cannot be destroyed. It must be stored somewhere, and no storage option is without risk. That risk is then present for at least hundreds of years and maybe more. Clearly, any policy of *not* developing a valley, of not building the road, and of not building nuclear power stations involves a forgone benefit.

One approach which goes some way towards solving these problems has been developed by Krutilla and Fisher (1975). Essentially what they propose is that, in cost-benefit analysis the *forgone benefit* resulting from the environmental loss in future years should be treated as a cost. Furthermore this cost can be expected to increase over time because (a) the demand for environmental services will increase and (b) the supply of such facilities is limited.

If the growth in the benefits forgone is sufficiently high, it will "cancel out" (at least to some extent) the effects of discounting future costs. In this way the losses from an irreversible change can be factored into conventional cost-benefit analysis with discounting.

3. Future generations

The question arises as to why market rates of discount are thought to be inappropriate in a context where the interests and rights of future generations are accepted as legitimate factors in the selection of a social discount rate. This section briefly surveys the arguments relating to this issue.

The higher the rate of discount the greater will be the discrimination against future generations. First, projects with social costs that occur well into the future and net social benefits that occur in the near term will be likelier to pass the standard cost-benefit test the higher the discount rate. Thus future generations may bear a disproportionate share of the costs of the project. Second, projects with social benefits well into the future are *less* likely to be favoured by the cost-benefit rule if discount rates are high. Thus future generations are denied a higher share of project benefits. Third, the higher the discount rate the lower will be the overall level of investment, depending on the availability of capital, and hence the lower the capital stock "inherited" by future generations. The expectation must be, then, that future generations will suffer from rates of discount determined in the market place since such rates are based on current generation preferences and/or capital productivity which is not associated with the general existence of future markets.

It might be thought, however, that existing preferences do take account of future generations' interests. The way in which this might occur is through "overlapping utility functions". What this means is that my welfare (utility) today includes as one of the factors determining it the welfare of my children and perhaps my grandchildren. In this way, we could argue that the "future generation's problem" is automatically taken account of in current preferences.

The basic reason for supposing that market rates do not reflect the interests of future generations is that they are determined by the behaviour of many individuals behaving in their own interest. If future generations enter into the calculus, they do so in contexts when the individual behaves in his or her "public role". The idea here is that we all make decisions in two contexts – "private" decisions reflecting our own interests, and "public" decisions in which we act with responsibility for our fellow beings and for future generations. Market discount rates reflect the former context, whereas social discount rates should reflect the public context. This is what some economists call the "dual role" rationale for social discount rates being below the market rates because of the future generations issue. It is also similar to the "assurance" argument, namely that people will behave differently if they can be assured that their own actions will be accompanied by similar actions by others. Thus, we might each be willing to make transfers to future generations, but only if we are individually assured that others will do the same. If we cannot be so assured, our transfers will be less. The "assured" discount rate arising from collective action is lower than the "unassured" discount rate.

There are other arguments that are used to justify the idea that market rates will be too high in the context of future generations' interests. One is the "super-responsibility" argument. Market discount rates arise from the behaviour of individuals, but the state is a separate entity with the responsibility of guarding collective welfare and the welfare of future generations as well. Thus, the rate of discount relevant to state investments will not be the same as the market discount rate and, since high rates discriminate against future generations, we would expect the state discount rate to be lower than the market discount rate.

This discussion suggests that the social discount rate should be used and that it is to be determined in the context of collective decision-making rather than some aggregation of individuals' decisions. This might mean looking at individuals' "public role" behaviour, leaving the choice of discount rate to the state, or trying to select a discount rate based on a collective saving contract. None of these options, however, offer a theory of how to determine a discount rate in quantitative terms. What they do suggest is that market rates will not be proper guides to discount rates once future generations' interests are incorporated into the social decision rule. The view taken is that these arguments can be used to justify rejecting the market rate of interest as a social discount rate *if it is thought that the burden of accounting for future generations' interests should fall on the discount rate.*

As we argue, however, we consider this an unnecessarily complex and almost certainly untenable procedure. It is better to define the rights of future generations and use these to circumscribe the overall cost-benefit rule, leaving the choice of discount rate to fairly conventional current-generation oriented considerations. A telling reason for this is that lowering rates will encourage more investment overall, and this will increase the demand for resources and environmental services. A lowering of rates across the board could thus have counterproductive results if the aim is to accommodate environmental concerns. One alternative, of course, is to lower discount rates for "environmental" projects, but not for other projects. In practice this is likely to be impossible to do because of the problems of deciding which is an environmental project and which is not. Is any rural development investment, for example, an environmental project? Since most projects will have an environmental dimension – they will all impact positively or negatively on the environment – the analyst would have to have some idea of the *scale* of the environmental dimension before deciding which discount rate to choose. Then he would need a cut-off point in order to decide which projects qualify for the lower rate and which for the higher one. Altogether, the procedure has large arbitrary features.

We suggest, then, that while there are attractive features in the future generations argument, they may either backfire in the sense of not accommodating the concerns that motivate a reduced discount rate, or they will result in largely impractical procedures.

How might future generations' interests be taken into account?

This, we suggest, is what the sustainable development criterion introduced in Chapter 2 and applied in Chapters 4, 5 and 7 does better than making adjustments to discount rates.

Conclusions

In this chapter we have shown that discount rates do not necessarily act to the detriment of the environment. A high rate reduces the overall level of investment, which means more natural areas are likely to be preserved and more environmentally desirable land use will be maintained. On the other hand, the higher the rate, the faster natural resources will be exploited and the less weight will be given to future costs of present projects. Thus the discount factor cuts in two different directions.

The basis of the discount rate lies in the social rate of time preference and in the opportunity cost of capital. Typically the latter implies a higher rate than the former. For *both*, however, there is a distinction between the "private" rate and the social rate. In general the social rate, from either perspective, will tend to be lower than the private rate.

Environmental concerns suggest that market rates should be adjusted to social rates. However, there are compelling arguments why this should not be done:

(i) calculating the appropriate rate is extremely difficult;
(ii) a lowering of the rate overall will result in more investment with its non-counter-productive results;
(iii) a selective lowering of the rate for environmental projects is inefficient and administratively cumbersome and difficult;
(iv) There are alternative ways of dealing with many of the environmental concerns that are probably more effective.

Instead of adjusting discount rates we recommend therefore that environmental efforts be concentrated on:

(i) *improving valuation* techniques, including valuing future costs and benefits more carefully;

(ii) *integrating environmental* considerations into *all* economic decisions; and
(iii) incorporating a *sustainability* constraint in the appraisal of environmental programmes, as suggested in Chapter 5.

Notes

1. This literature is reviewed in Anil Markandya and David Pearce, *Environmental Considerations and the Choice of Discount Rate in Developing Countries*, Environment Department Working Paper No. 3, World Bank, Washington, DC, May 1988.
2. The 5 per cent rate is now out of line with private-sector returns and is under review. On pure SOC grounds, one would expect the rate to be raised.

7. PRICES AND INCENTIVES FOR ENVIRONMENTAL IMPROVEMENT

Levels of the economy at which sustainable development incentives are required

Chapter 4 indicated ways in which sustainable development might be monitored at the *macroeconomic* level by supporting the existing national income accounts with additional environmental accounts. Such macroeconomic monitoring is not itself an *instrument* of sustainable development policy, but it is a precondition for rational policy.

Chapter 5 showed that sustainable development policy could be implemented at the *macroeconomic and sectoral level* by shifting the balance of capital investment between environmentally damaging and environmentally augmenting activities. This involved (a) considering the overall portfolio of public sector investment, the portfolio of investments available to any single agency *and* (c) ensuring that *project appraisal* within a sector or agency is carried out in such a way that environmental values are properly represented.

Chapter 6 looked at one of the *prices* that affect investment decisions – the *discount rate*. For the discount rate can be thought of as a price of present against future consumption: it is an "intertemporal price". The argument in Chapter 6 was that the discount rate used for public sector projects could indeed be altered to reflect environmental values and to reflect better the interests of future generations, two of the "basic ingredients" of sustainable development. But, for analytical and pragmatic reasons, it was suggested that changing the discount rate would probably not be the most efficient way of reflecting sustainable development concerns in project planning. A preferable route to integrating sustainability into project appraisal is (a) to ensure that environmental values are fully and properly reflected in the appraisals and (b) to adopt some form of "compensating project" approach in order to maintain environmental assets over time.

This chapter now addresses the remaining economic instrument for ensuring sustainable development, the *prices* of goods and services and resources.[1]

Markets and prices

The most desirable feature of the price mechanism is that it signals to consumers what the cost of producing a particular product is, and to producers what consumers' relative valuations are. In a nutshell, this is the elegance and virtue of free markets which economists have (generally) found so attractive since the time of Adam Smith.

As Chapter 1 noted, however, many environmental products, services and resources do not get represented in the price mechanism. This effectively amounts to them being treated as "free goods", i.e. they have zero prices. It follows that an *unfettered* price mechanism will use too much of the zero-priced good. Resources and environments will become degraded on this basis alone, i.e. because the price mechanism has wrongly recorded environmental goods as having zero prices when, in fact, they serve economic functions which should attract positive prices.

But economic goods and services themselves "use up" some of the environment. Trace gases "use" the atmosphere and troposphere as a waste sink; municipalities use rivers and coastal waters as cleansing agents for sewage, and so on. The cost of producing any good or service therefore tends to be a mixture of priced "inputs" (labour, capital, technology) and unpriced inputs (environmental services). The market price for goods and services does not therefore reflect the true value of the totality of the resources being used to produce them. Unfettered markets fail to allocate resources efficiently. Or, in the economists' language, there is a divergence between private and social cost.

There are of course, ways in which freely functioning "unfettered" markets will achieve improvements in environmental quality. If consumers change their tastes in favour of less polluting products and against more polluting forces, market forces will lead to a change in the "pollution content" of final products and services. This is the "green consumerism" argument. For green consumerism to be effective consumers must be *informed* about the pollution profile of the products they buy. Government has a role, with other agencies, in extending the amount and quality of this information.

Green consumerism may do little to alter *production processes* since the consumer (a) is generally less well informed about these processes and (b) is less able to impact on the choice of process. Process changes will occur if industry also becomes environmentally conscious, and/or the cost signals to industry alter.

There are two ways in which markets can be restructured so as to ensure that environmental services enter into the market system more effectively.

First, we could create markets in previously free services: all natural areas could charge entrance fees, coastal zones could be placed under private ownership with the owners charging for the use of coastal waters as sewage dumps, and so on. This is the *full privatization* option.

Second, we could "modify" markets by centrally deciding the value of the environmental services and ensuring that those values are incorporated into the prices of goods and services. We refer to this regulatory approach as using the market, or establishing *market-based incentives*.

In what follows we explore the latter option and not the former. Apart from our terms of reference, the rationale here is simply that many environmental functions cannot be handed over to private ownership – the ozone layer, the oceans, the atmosphere are examples. Moreover, a market-based system of regulation can be shown to be more efficient than one based on "command-and-control", i.e. one which simply sets environmental standards and enforces them without the aid of market-based incentives.

How then would a market-based incentive system work so as to contribute to sustainable development?

The proper pricing of products and services

Once the divergence between private and social costs of production is accepted, it follows logically that the "proper" price for products and services is one that reflects the wider social costs of production, inclusive of any environmental services. Economists have shown that *if there is no divergence between private and social cost* then a free market works best – i.e. it achieves the most efficient allocation of resources – if prices reflect the cost of producing an extra unit of output, the so-called "marginal cost" (MC). In light of the discussion about the value of environmental services this rule needs to be modified to setting prices so that they reflect "marginal *social* cost" (MSC).[2]

For any product that imposes pollution damage on a third party, this rule amounts to saying that the product being produced should have a price (P) in the market of:

$$P = MC + MEC = MSC$$

where MEC is the marginal pollution damage expressed in money terms, or the "marginal external cost".

The more competitive the market the closer P is likely to be to MC, but, as we have noted, there is no incentive for the market to reflect MEC in the price formula. Accordingly, actual prices will diverge from MSC by the amount MEC. Put another way, the prices of polluting products will be too low in the free market. There is a need to correct the market prices by *making the polluter pay* the extra amount (MEC).

Making the polluter pay

The *Polluter Pays Principle* is now fairly familiar in policy circles. The OECD Council set the principle out in 1974 (see Box 7.1).

As interpreted by OECD the Polluter Pays Principle (PPP) is broader than is suggested by the argument above. For, strictly, to secure an efficient allocation of resources, product prices should reflect MSC where the MEC component of MSC has been evaluated in monetary terms. Procedures for securing

Box 7.1   **The Polluter Pays Principle: OECD's interpretation**

A. GUIDING PRINCIPLES

Cost Allocation: the Polluter Pays Principle

1. Environmental resources are in general limited and their use in production and consumption activities may lead to their deterioration. When the cost of this deterioration is not adequately taken into account in the price system, the market fails to reflect the scarcity of such resources both at the national and international levels. Public measures are thus necessary to reduce pollution and to reach a better allocation of resources by ensuring that prices of goods depending on the quality and/or quantity of environmental resource reflect more closely their relative scarcity and that economic agents concerned react accordingly.

2. In many circumstances, in order to ensure that the environment is in an acceptable state, the reduction of pollution beyond a certain level will not be practical or even necessary in view of the costs involved.

3. The principle to be used for allocating costs of pollution prevention and control measures to encourage rational use of scarce environmental resources and to avoid distortions in international trade and investment is the so-called "Polluter Pays Principle". This principle means that the environment is in an acceptable state. In other words, the cost of these measures should be reflected in the cost of goods and services which cause pollution in production and/or consumption. Such measures should not be accompanied by subsidies that would create significant distortions in international trade and investment.

4. This principle should be an objective of member countries; however, there may be exceptions or special arrangements, particularly for the transitional periods, provided that they do not lead to significant distortions in international trade and investment.

Source: OECD, *The Polluter Pays Principle: Definition, Analysis, Implementation* (Paris: OECD, 1975).

such monetary evaluations are given in Chapter 3. In practice, monetary evaluations may be difficult to carry out, and there has always been some opposition to the idea of putting money values on the environment. Moreover, the economic efficiency interpretation of PPP assumes that society aims to achieve the "optimal" level of pollution,[3] whereas in practice it is more feasible to think and design policy in terms of "acceptable" levels of pollution. Accordingly, the OECD PPP is formulated in broader terms of making the polluter bear the costs of standard-setting. What this means is that a standard for "acceptable" environmental quality is set and the polluter is obliged, in the first instance, to pay the necessary costs of getting to that standard. The standard may or may not correspond to the economist's definition of the "optimal" level of pollution. Indeed, it is very unlikely to correspond to it other than by accident.

The basic mechanisms for making the polluter pay are:

(i) by setting *standards*, the cost of achieving which is initially borne by the producer;
(ii) by setting *charges* or *taxes* on the polluting product or input;
(iii) by setting a standard, issuing *pollution permits* in amounts consistent with the standard, and allowing those permits to be *traded*.

Who is the polluter?

Note that the PPP speaks of making the *polluter* pay. But, as with any cost increase, if polluters can pass on an increase in the cost of production to *consumers*, they will do so. In practice they can pass on only *part* of the increased costs they bear. Box 7.2 shows why.

Making the consumer of the polluting product pay some of the clean-up cost may seem at odds with the PPP but in fact it is exactly what should happen. For the price mechanism now signals the "true" costs of production to the consumer, comprising normal costs of production *and* the hitherto free environmental inputs. That is how the "green power of market forces" works.[4]

Box 7.2 **Producers and consumers are the polluters: sharing the cost of pollution control**

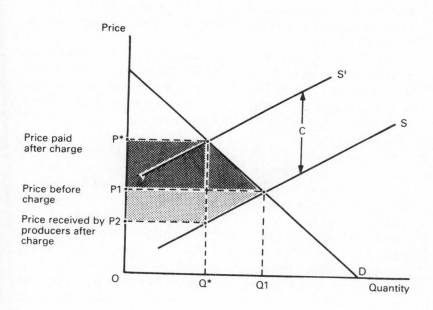

The diagram shows a supply curve, S, and a demand curve D. A pollution charge, C, is put into effect, raising producers' costs and causing the supply curve to rise to S'. The new market price is P*. Consumers pay this price in the market, but out of it producers must pay the charge component C, so the price received by producers is actually only P2. Producers have borne some of the cost of the charge (a measure of their loss is the light shaded area in the diagram), but so have consumers (a measure of their loss is the heavy shaded area). What the exact relative contributions of producer and consumer are depends on the slopes of the S and D curves. Generally, the more competition there is in the market between producers, the less will consumers bear the burden of a pollution charge.

Sustainable development and the PPP

Sustainable development can be furthered by acceptance of the PPP, for the PPP enables the market to be adjusted in such a way that the true costs of producing goods and services are reflected in prices. The relevance of the PPP to achieving sustainable development should not be underestimated, for the price mechanism is a powerful means of allocating resources in the economy.

But all OECD member nations already adhere to the PPP as formulated by OECD. The issue has therefore to be whether that adherence, as reflected in national environmental policies, is adequate to achieve sustainable development. There are strong reasons for thinking that existing policies will not suffice.

Much of the thinking about sustainable development emerged because of the environmental challenges of the end of the twentieth century and the prospective challenges of the twenty-first. Some of those challenges are global – climate change and ozone layer reduction; some are international – transboundary "acid rain" for example; some are national – coastal waters pollution in many cases, loss of habitat. Thus, even if it was possible to argue that *past* policies have been adequate to handle past and current policies, and many would dispute that, the pressing issue is whether a "trends continued" approach will be sufficient. Suppose that even this is thought to be the case, i.e. that there is no great need to reformulate the existing *general* approach to environmental policy in light of sustainable development considerations. (Again, many would doubt this.) Then it is enough to observe that the *cost* of environmental policy will rise, particularly if there is to be a serious attempt to tackle the major global issues. And if the cost is expected to rise, then it is irrational to adopt the most expensive way of tackling future environmental policies. The prospect of a rising cost of environmental protection ought to focus attention on the use of the market-based incentives. For such incentives can be demonstrated to minimise the real costs of achieving a given environmental standard.

To avoid the risk of misunderstanding: what is being argued

here is that, *given* an environmental quality objective, the aim of society should be to achieve that standard at minimum cost. This is wholly consistent with the idea of sustainable development since it both ensures that acceptable environmental standards are achieved *and* avoids wasting resources on expensive approaches when cheaper ones will suffice. What is saved is then available to devote to the other development objectives.[5]

What are market-based incentives?

Pollution charges/taxes. Market-based incentives are almost self-explanatory: they are incentive systems that operate, generally through establishing *prices* for environmental services, via a market. The markets in question are either established ones, for example existing markets in goods and services or in labour and capital equipment. Or the market may be "created", usually with some form of encouragement from government.

The simplest conceptual form of a market-based incentive is the *pollution charge or tax*. Essentially what happens here is that a charge is set on the product (or the inputs used to make the product) so as to raise the cost of producing the product. The charge should then bear some relationship to the value of the environmental services used in production. Ideally, the charge would equal the value of MEC in the basic price equation established previously. But it is also the case that even where the PPP is modified to mean that the polluter bears the initial cost of meeting a pre-ordained standard, a charge can be very useful. Above all, it can be shown that charges often produce lower compliance costs – the costs that polluters bear in meeting the standard – than would be the case if the standard was simply set and polluters were legally obliged to honour it however best they see fit.[6]

The basic reason why charges are likely to be better than "command-and-control" techniques is that charges enable a polluter to choose how to adjust to the environmental quality standard. Polluters with high costs of abating pollution will prefer to pay the charge. Polluters with low costs of abatement will prefer to install abatement equipment. By making abatement something that "low cost" polluters do rather than "high cost" ones, charges tend to cut down the total costs of compliance.

Note, once again, there is no question of the charging mechanism reducing the environmental quality standard. It is the *same* standard as would be achieved by command-and-control. The charge simply introduces flexibility into the compliance mechanism. Command-and-control, because of its rigidities, does not do this.

The first proposition, then, is that pollution charges are generally better than "command-and-control". Such a blanket statement disguises many problems with taxes, but for current purposes the general implication is correct. A tax adjusts market prices to reflect the use of environmental services which are otherwise erroneously treated as being free. Command-and-control policies adopt a regulatory stance which ignores the efficiencies of the market mechanism.

Box 7.3 illustrates some charging mechanisms currently in place in OECD countries. Charges are made on effluents in a number of countries; on noise nuisance in some instances in quite a number of countries; on the collection and disposal of wastewater in virtually all countries studied; on products (such as bottle deposit systems) in quite a number of countries; and differential taxes are used in a few countries. The *idea* of charging is not new, therefore. But the authors of the survey from which Box 7.3 is taken are clear in concluding that the charges in question are *not* designed for incentive purposes, or, if they were intended to be, they do not have significant incentive effects. Many, for example, are for revenue-raising which is an altogether different objective.

The message here is that charges should be used to provide incentives for polluters to abate pollution.

A carbon tax

A tax on carbon fuels is widely discussed as a means of combatting global warming through the release of greenhouse

Box 7.3 Charging mechanisms in OECD countries

Country	Air	Effluent		Noise	User	Product	Administrative	Tax differentiation
		Water	Waste					
Australia		□	□			□	□	
Belgium		□				□	□	
Canada						□		
Denmark					□	□	□	□
Finland					□	□	□	□
France	□	□		□	□	□		
German		□		□	□	□	□	
Italy		□			□	□		
Japan	□			□				
Netherlands	□	□	□	□	□	□	□	□
Norway					□	□	□	□
Sweden					□	□	□	□
Switzerland					□	□		□
United Kingdom					□	□	□	
United States	□		□		□		□	

Source: J.B. Opschoor and H. Vos, *The Application of Economic Instruments for Environmental Protection in OECD Member Countries* (Paris: OECD, 1988).

gases. A carbon tax would be graduated according to the carbon content of fuels. Thus coal would attract a higher tax than oil which in turn would attract a higher tax than natural gas. Electricity would not be taxed directly but would pay the taxes on the carbon fuels. In this way the electricity sector would alter its fuel mix to a less carbon-polluting form.

As noted above, any tax on an input such as fuel will be partly borne by producers, partly by consumers. This is consistent with the PPP.

What is the effect on consumers? If consumers have a choice of heating systems for households one would expect some substitution of less polluting heating systems (e.g. gas) for more polluting systems (e.g. oil). Many households, however, are "locked in" to existing heating technologies. The effect of a carbon tax on these consumers, as on those who have a choice of systems, is to encourage conservation, i.e. the reduction in the total amount of energy consumed.

Thus, a carbon tax would encourage

(i) a switch in the fuel mix of the industrial and electricity sector;

(ii) a switch in the fuel mix of the household sector;

(iii) energy conservation in all energy-using sectors.

These advantages of a carbon tax need to be set against possible disadvantages. First, an energy tax tends to be regressive in so far as the poor and aged respond less in terms of energy conservation than do the better off and younger sections of society. But many taxes are regressive and mechanisms to offset the regressiveness do exist, e.g. through other tax or benefit concessions.

Second, a carbon tax may appear to add to the tax base of the taxing country. New taxes tend to be treated with suspicion. One possibility for encouraging wider acceptance is to couple the carbon tax with reductions in other taxes. A carbon tax associated with other tax offsets obviously generates no gain in net revenue to government, but it still serves the important function of correcting the resource misallocation arising from the failure to charge the full social cost of energy use.

Third, a carbon tax *in one country alone* is likely to have negligible impact on the problem of global warming. The reasons for this are that (a) carbon gases are only one of the gases contributing to the "greenhouse effect" (CO_2 maybe accounts for 50 per cent of all greenhouse gases), and (b) any one country tends to contribute small amounts to the overall CO_2 global emission level. A third possible reason for limited impact would arise if the demand for energy is "price inelastic", i.e. if demand is comparatively unresponsive to price. This suggests that a carbon tax is one instrument for consideration in a *global convention* on carbon emissions.

The principles underlying a carbon tax are the same for any energy source: the full social costs of energy use should be reflected in the price of energy. The greenhouse gas problem is only one environmental issue. "Acid rain" pollution tends to reinforce the idea of taxing carbon fuels. In the same way, while nuclear power is free of a carbon tax, its own social costs need to be reflected in electricity prices. Such costs include waste disposal, decommissioning, routine radiation and the costs of accidents.

Creating markets. But markets can also be created. One way of doing this is to establish a pre-ordained environmental standard and then issue "permits" for polluters. Such an idea strikes many as immoral, but it is exactly what happens with the command-and-control system anyway. Polluters are "permitted" to pollute up to a certain level and then no more. The idea of a "pollution permit" therefore ought not to occasion any concern unless the doubt is about the ability of the authorities to set "acceptable" quality standards – and that doubt exists whatever method of control is sought. The next stage is to establish a market in the permits – that is to allow them to be bought and sold. The rationale for this is the same as that underlying the pollution charges approach: polluters with high abatement costs will prefer to buy the permits, while low abatement cost polluters will sell permits in favour of abating pollution. Once again, the overall standard is not threatened, for that is determined by the authorities and they set the number of permits accordingly. Moreover, if they wish to tighten standards they can "buy in" the permits themselves and reduce their number, thus reducing the "permitted" amount of pollution.

We conclude that marketable permits offer a further market-based incentive system to meet pre-ordained environmental quality standards at lower cost.

Some experience of marketable permits exists in the USA. Box 7.4 produces some important evidence about the cost-saving features of the permit system. The evidence relates to the US experience with air pollution emissions trading. The terminology is explained in the illustration. The effect of emissions trading on the quality of the environment is not regarded by the authors as having been significant. This is not a major criticism of emissions trading: a command-and-control system

Box 7.4   **Saving pollution control costs with marketable permits**

EMISSIONS TRADING ACTIVITY (CUMULATIVE ESTIMATES THROUGH 1985)

	Bubbles		Offsets	Netting	Banking
	Federal	State			
Number of trades	42	90	1,000	8,000	100
Cost savings (millions)	$300	$135	N/A	$4,000	very small
Air quality impact	neutral	neutral	neutral	slightly negative	very slightly positive

The gains in terms of reduced compliance costs come from EPA's policy of "netting", "offsets", "bubbles" and "banking". Netting (introduced in 1974) allows a firm creating a new emissions source within a plant to reduce emissions from another source within the plant so long as the *net* emissions do not increase significantly. Effectively the firm is allowed to *trade* with itself. Offsets (introduced in 1976) relate to new emission sources in areas which have so far failed to achieve their standards ("nonattainment" areas). A new emissions source will be allowed in such areas only if another source achieves reduced emissions by a larger amount. Offsets can be achieved by "internal" trading within the firm *or* by trading with another firm – "external trading". Bubbles were introduced in 1979 and similarly allow sources to offset each other as long as the total emissions do not increase. However, bubbles relate to *existing sources*. Banking, introduced in 1979, allows a firm to "save" any "credits" it gets by reducing emissions to permit emissions at some time in the future.

Source: Robert Hahn and Gordon Hester, "The Market for Bads", *Regulation*, Nos. 3/4, 1987.

would be unlikely to have fared any better. The critical point is that the emissions trading system reduced the costs of compliance with the standards. The authors of the study underlying Box 7.4 conclude: "The performance of emissions trading confirms economists' predictions that market-based approaches to pollution control can be highly cost-effective."[7]

The proper pricing of natural resources

The theory of marginal social cost pricing is just as applicable to natural resource use. Any natural resource should be priced so that the price reflects the (marginal) cost of extraction or harvesting and the marginal external cost (MEC) of any damage done by using the resource. For an exhaustible resource, however, there is an additional component to price. This arises because, by definition, removal and use of a unit of the resource now means that it is not available for the future. The easiest examples to think of are coal and oil. Effectively, current use precludes future use. The associated cost is termed "user cost".[8] We could then write the formula for the "proper" pricing of a natural resource as:

$$P = MC + MEC + MUC = MOC$$

We have given the name *marginal opportunity cost* to this pricing rule. Note that if resource extraction does not incur external costs and if there are reasons for thinking MUC is very small, then the pricing rule would be approximately achieved by a competitive market. Indeed, it can be argued that MUC will be reflected in current prices – that depends on how far current markets reflect future scarcity, an issue that is debated among economists.

However, for many resources the MEC component will be significant. An example would be the climatic impacts of coal burning, accident hazards from nuclear power stations, oil spills from tanker and platform accidents, and so on.

Integrative environmental policy and market-based incentives

The nature of the interactions between economies and natural environments is sufficient to establish that waste products are *pervasive* to economic systems.[9] The policy implication of this observation is that "containment" in one environmental medium can quickly result in the problem reappearing in another medium. Indeed, this problem has been acknowledged by the UK government:

> The last few years have seen a rapid growth in understanding
> of the inter-related nature of our environment . . . . This has
> led to the widespread appreciation that tighter standards in any
> one environmental medium generate pressures on the other
> media.[10]

There is a distinct role for market-based incentives in ensuring integrated pollution control. For once the principle of using markets to deal with pollution policy is established there are several ways of reflecting the integrated nature of that policy in the economic instruments being used. It would mean for example that a charge or permit system could be established for, say, products and resources which result in airborne emissions. If resource users have alternative options for disposal, e.g. by land or water disposal, then it will be important to extend the charge or permit system to those media as well.[11] In the case of charges, the charge should be higher the more damage is likely to be done. Thus, a firm emitting air pollutants may do a certain amount of damage, but would do greater damage if it "switched" to a water media waste emission process. The charge for disposing of waste to water would then need to be higher than that for the air media emissions. In much the same way, the quantity of permits could be varied according to the "sensitivity" of the media receiving wastes.

The important point is that market-based incentives cannot be established "in isolation" in contexts where it is possible to switch waste emissions from one receiving medium to another.

None the less, the USA experience already establishes that there are cost savings to be made even where market-based incentives are applied to a single medium.

Incentives and energy conservation

The role of incentives and environmental quality can be illustrated in the important context of international and global air quality. "Acid rain" and global warming are linked to airborne emissions from fossil fuel burning, and, within that contribution, electricity production has a significant role. Self-evidently, reductions in fuel consumption will contribute at source to reductions in emissions. It seems likely that *energy conservation* could play the largest role in securing those reductions in emissions. Indeed, over the last 100 years, the energy required for producing a single "unit" of GNP has declined systematically. Originally this was because the UK began to switch out of heavy industry and into less energy-intensive manufacturing and then service industries. In the 1970s the trend was given a boost by high energy prices. Yet, these long-run factors and prices apart, many energy consumers seem reluctant to invest in energy conservation. There is an economic rationale for supposing that markets are not working effectively to secure the "right" amount of energy conservation.

There are three reasons why markets in energy conservation "fail":

- prices do not reflect the true "social cost" of production;
- consumers have high discount rates;
- consumers have poor information.

If energy conservation is to be advanced in order to tackle acid rain and the greenhouse gas problem, policy must be directed at all three "failures". Yet the UK has invested significantly in information campaigns, which suggests that the focus of conservation policy needs to shift to the price and discount rate problem.

Prices need to reflect both the "internal" costs of electricity production and the "external" costs. Reflecting private costs properly (marginal rather than average costs) is something that UK electricity production probably does, and as the retrofit of coal-fired stations takes place with FGD equipment, so more of the external cost element is being absorbed also. But there is clearly further scope for making the full social cost element more prominent.

Empirical work suggests that consumers of electricity (and

energy in general) often have very high discount rates, suggesting that in any rational weighing up of the costs and benefits of conservation to them they will under-invest in conservation compared to what is socially desirable. Indeed, some studies show that poorer and older consumers may have rates of discount of over 80 per cent (compare this to the 10–14 per cent market borrowing rates, or the 25–30 per cent on credit-card borrowing). Young, wealthier consumers have been found to have low rates.

The implications for market incentives are that conservation policy might need to be targeted according to who the consumer is. A policy of subsidies to the older and poorer, for example, would have an economic justification in this context. Information and "environmental awareness" campaigns would be better directed to the young.

This discussion is illustrative only. Clearly, actual policy design would need to be based on full research.

Conclusions on pricing for sustainable development

The economic principles underlying the "proper" pricing of goods and services and of natural resources are the same. Prices should reflect the true social costs of production and use. Essentially this means getting the true values of environmental services reflected in prices, rather than having them treated as "free goods".

Price is a powerful weapon in the pursuit of the environmental policies needed for sustainable development because it allows resource users to respond in the same way as they do to price signals elsewhere in the market. Using prices in this way is wholly consistent with the "polluter pays" principle which the UK already supports. But there are powerful reasons for arguing that the traditional "standard-setting" approach to environmental policy now needs to be supplemented by more market-based approaches, using charges and tradeable permits. Not least among the reasons for this redirection of choice of policy instrument is the impending increased cost of achieving environmental quality if a systematic and forceful approach to the "new" international and global environmental problems is to take place.

Notes

1. The focus of this report is on the *economic* implications of sustainable development. This should not obscure the fact that there are political, social and institutional implications.
2. For the analytics of securing "optimality" by setting prices everywhere equal to marginal social costs see any standard welfare economics text, e.g. Richard Just, Darrell Hueth and Andrew Schmitz, *Applied Welfare Economics and Public Policy* (New Jersey: Prentice-Hall, 1982).
3. The "optimal" level of pollution in terms of economic efficiency is that level of pollution that would arise if prices were everywhere set equal to MSC.
4. The phrase is Samuel Brittan's, see "The green power of market forces", *Financial Times*, 4 May 1989.
5. The explanation is necessary because mention of "least cost" approaches to achieving acceptable environmental quality tends to evoke reactions of achieving environmental quality "on the cheap", as if, in some way, it is the quality objective that will be sacrificed.
6. The formal proof of this proposition is due to William Baumol and William Oates, "The uses of standards and prices for protection of the environment", *Swedish Journal of Economics*, March 1971.
7. From Robert Hahn and Gordon Hester, "The market for bads: EPA's experience with emissions trading", *Regulation*, Nos 3/4, 1987.
8. A reasonably straightforward formula for estimating marginal user cost is that it is equal to

$$(P_B - C)/(1 + r)^T$$

where P_B is the price of the technology that would substitute for the resource eventually (nuclear power for coal, say, or shale oil for sea-bed oil), C is the cost of extraction of the resource which will be substituted, r is the discount rate and T is the time by which the backstop technology comes into play. See David Pearce and R Kerry Turner, *Economics of Natural Resources and the Environment* (London: Simon & Schuster, 1989), ch.18.

9. This simply reflects the materials "throughput" to the economic system, some of which can be recycled, and the one-way energy throughput, since energy cannot be recycled. In environmental economics this interaction is summed up as the *materials balance principle* which basically says that whatever resources flow into the economic system must reappear somewhere else in that system as wastes.

10. UK Department of the Environment and Welsh Office, *Integrated Pollution Control: a Consultation Paper*, London, July 1988.

11. The UK government has already proposed a very limited form of charging to recover the costs of Her Majesty's Inspectorate of Pollution in so far as they relate to control of pollution by firms. This is related to the general principle enunciated in the text, but, of course, we are considering charging for the *damage* done. See Department of the Environment and Welsh Office, *Cost Recovery Charging for Integrated Pollution Control*, London, April 1989.

ANNEX: SUSTAINABLE DEVELOPMENT – A GALLERY OF DEFINITIONS

While a great deal has been written about sustainable development, it is difficult to find rigorous definitions of it. The following selection illustrates various perspectives on sustainable development out of which we have derived our general definition in Chapter 2.

"Sustainable development – development that is likely to achieve lasting satisfaction of human needs and improvement of the quality of human life." (p.23)

Robert Allen, *How to Save The World* (London: Kogan Page, 1980), summarizing *The World Conservation Strategy*.

"The concept of sustainable economic development as applied to the Third World . . . is therefore directly concerned with increasing the material standard of living of the poor at the 'grassroots' level, which can be quantitatively measured in terms of increased food, real income, educational services, health-care, sanitation and water supply, emergency stocks of food and cash, etc., and only indirectly concerned with economic growth at the aggregate, commonly national, level. In general terms, the primary objective is reducing the absolute poverty of the world's poor through providing lasting and secure livelihoods that minimize resource depletion, environmental degradation, cultural disruption and social instability." (p.103)

Edward Barbier, "The Concept of Sustainable Economic Development", *Environmental Conservation*, Vol.14 (No.2), 1987, pp.101-110.

"A broad consensus does exist about the conditions required for sustainable economic development. Two interpretations are now emerging: a wider concept concerned with sustainable economic, ecological and social development; and a more narrowly defined concept largely concerned with environmentally sustainable development (i.e., with optimal resource and environmental management over time).

The wider, highly normative view of sustainable development (endorsed by the World Commission on Environment and Development) defines the concept as "development that meets the needs of the present without compromising the ability of future generations to meet their own needs."

In contrast, concern with optimal resource and environmental management over time – the more narrowly defined concept of environmentally sustainable development – requires maximizing the net benefits of economic development, subject to maintaining the services and quality of natural resources."

Edward Barbier, *Economics, Natural Resources, Scarcity and Development* (London: Earthscan, 1989).

"The World Commission does *not* believe that a *dismal* scenario of mounting destruction of national global potential for development – indeed, of the earth's capacity to support life – is an *inescapable destiny*. The problems are *planetary* – but they are not *insoluble*. I believe that history will record that in this crisis the two greatest resources, land and people, will redeem the promise of development. *If we take care of nature, nature will take care of us*. Conservation has truly come of age when it acknowledges that if we want to save *part* of the system we have to save the *system itself*. This is the essence of what we call *sustainable development*.

There are many dimensions to sustainability. First, it requires the elimination of poverty and deprivation. Second, it requires the conservation and enhancement of the resources base which alone can ensure that the elimination of the poverty is permanent. Third, it requires a broadening of the concept of development so that it covers not only economic growth but also social and cultural development. Fourth, and *most* important, it requires the unification of economics and ecology in decision-making at all levels."

Prime Minister Gro Harlem Brundtland, Sir Peter Scott Lecture, Bristol, 8 October 1986.

"A major challenge of the coming decades is to learn how long-term large-scale interactions between environment and development can be better managed to increase the prospects for ecologically sustainable improvements in human well-being." (p.5)

W. Clark and R. Munn, *Sustainable Development of the Biosphere*, (Cambridge: Cambridge University Press, 1986).

"More difficult to define is sustainability. The common use of the word 'sustainable' suggests an ability to maintain some activity in the face of stress – for example to sustain physical exercise, such as jogging or doing press-ups – and this seems to us also the most technically acceptable meaning. We thus define agricultural sustainability as the ability to maintain productivity, whether of a field or farm or nation, in the face of stress or shock." (p.653)

Gordon Conway and Edward Barbier, "After the Green Revolution: Sustainable and Equitable Agricultural Development", *Futures*, (20), No.6, December 1988.

"[The] sustainable society is one that lives within the self-perpetuating limits of its environment. That society . . . is not a 'no-growth' society . . . . It is, rather, a society that recognizes the limits of growth . . . [and] looks for alternative ways of growing."

James Coomer, "The Nature of the Quest for a Sustainable Society", in J. Coomer (ed.), *Quest for a Sustainable Society* (Oxford: Pergamon Press, 1979).

"Sustainable development is here defined as a pattern of social and structural economic transformations (i.e. 'development') which optimizes the economic and societal benefits available in the present, without jeopardizing the likely potential for similar benefits in the future. A primary goal of sustainable development is to achieve a reasonable (however defined) and equitably distributed level of economic well-being that can be perpetuated continually for many human generations."

" . . . sustainable development implies using renewable natural resources in a manner which does not eliminate or degrade them, or otherwise diminish their usefulness for future generations . . . . Sustainable development further implies using non-renewable (exhaustible) mineral resources in a manner which does not unnecessarily preclude easy access to them by future generations . . . . Sustainable development also implies depleting non-renewable energy resources at a slow enough rate so as to ensure the high probability of an orderly societal transition to renewable energy sources . . . "

Robert Goodland and G. Ledoc, "Neoclassical Economics and Principles of Sustainable Development", *Ecological Modelling*, Vol. 38, 1987.

"Guidelines for a responsible natural resources policy"

. . . activities should be considered that would be aimed at maintaining over time a constant effective natural resource base. This concept was proposed by Page (1977) and implies not an unchanging resource base but a set of resource reserves, technologies, and policy controls that maintain or expand the production possibilities of future generations."

Charles Howe, *Natural Resource Economics* (New York: Wiley, 1979).

"The basic idea [of sustainable development] is simple in the context of natural resources (excluding exhaustibles) and environments: the use made of these inputs to the development process should be sustainable through time . . . . If we now apply the idea to resources, sustainability ought to mean that a given stock of resources – trees, soil quality, water and so on – should not decline."

" . . . sustainability might be redefined in terms of a requirement that the use of resources today should not reduce real incomes in the future . . . . "

Anil Markandya and David Pearce, "Natural Environments and the Social Rate of Discount", *Project Appraisal*, Vol.3 (No.1), 1988.

"What should UNCTAD do to make development sustainable? It would be well on the way to reduce the international inertia that hinders sustainable development if it took some of the actions mentioned below. UNCTAD should:

– include environmental issues as an item on its agenda.
– give more attention to the concepts of 'environment' and 'sustainable development'.
– study in detail relationships between environment and development, and between growth and natural resources utilization. What are the effects of different development strategies on the environment? Is growth possible without severe exploitation of global natural resources? Can donor countries and international organizations make it a condition that future assistance not be used for activities that damage the environment?
– introduce a new goal for development, a better environment,

by using a longer perspective on developmental issues. Better use of natural resources is already an object of negotiations.
- take account of environmental requirements and sustainable development on every level of negotiations.
- establish a special committee or working group on environmental issues. Sustainable development can be discussed in all existent committees and working groups, especially in the Committee on Commodities.
- provide information to other international actors, initiate and co-ordinate international actions, and follow up implementa-,tion actions concerning environment and sustainable development."

Tuija Meisaari-Polsa, "UNCTAD and Sustainable Development – A Case Study of Difficulties in Large International Organisations", in Stockholm Group for Studies on Natural Resources Development, *Perspectives on Sustainable Development*, Stockholm Group for Studies on Natural Resources Management, Stockholm, 1988.

"Thus we need to nail down the concept of sustainable development. I propose five increasingly comprehensive definitions. First, we can start at the local level and simply ask whether a region's agricultural and industrial practices can continue indefinitely. Will they destroy the local resource base and environment or, just as bad, the local people and their cultural system? Or will the resource base, environment, technologies and culture evolve over time in a mutually reinforcing manner? This first definition ignores whether there might be subsidies to the region – whether material and energy inputs or social inputs such as the provision of new knowledge, technologies and institutional services are being supplied from outside the region.

Second, we can ask whether the region is dependent upon non-renewable inputs, both energy and materials, from beyond its boundaries. Or is the region dependent on renewable resources beyond its boundaries which are not being managed in a sustainable manner? Third, we can become yet more sophisticated and ponder whether the region is in some sense culturally sustainable, whether it is contributing as much to the knowledge and institutional bases of other regions as it is culturally dependent upon others. Fourth, we can also question the extent to which the region is contributing to global climate change, forcing other regions to change their behaviour, as well as whether it has options available to adapt to the climate change and surprises imposed upon it by others. From a global perspective, this fourth definition of sustainable development addresses the difficulties of going from hydrocarbon energy stocks to renewable energy sources while adapting to the complications of global climate change induced by the transitional net oxidation of hydrocarbons. Fifth, and last, we can inquire of the cultural stability of all the regions in combination, are they evolving along mutually compatible paths, or will they destroy each other through war?

These definitions become increasingly encompassing. All, however, address the sustainability of changing interactions between people and their environment over time."

Richard Norgaard, "Sustainable Development: a Co-Evolutionary View", *Futures*, Vol.20, No.6, December 1988.

"The sustainability criterion requires that the conditions necessary for equal access to the resource base be met for each generation."

David Pearce, "Foundations of an Ecological Economics", *Ecological Modelling*, Vol.38, 1987.

"In simple terms [sustainable development] argues for (a) development subject to a set of constraints which set resource harvest rates at levels no higher than managed or natural regeneration rates; and (b) use of the environment as a 'waste sink' on the basis that waste disposal rates should not exceed rates of (natural or managed) assimilation by the counterpart ecosystems . . . . There are self-evident problems in advocating sustainable rates for exhaustible resources, so that 'sustainabilists' tend to think in terms of a resource set encompassing substitution between renewables and exhaustibles. Equally self-evident is the implicit assumption that sustainability is a 'good thing' – that is optimising *within* sustainable use rates is a desirable objective. On these terms, sustainability could imply use of environmental services over very long time periods and, in theory, indefinitely."

David Pearce, "Optimal Prices for Sustainable Development". In D. Collard, D. Pearce and D. Ulph (eds), *Economics, Growth and Sustainable Environment* (London: Macmillan, 1988).

"The key concept [regarding natural resource degradation in developing countries] is 'sustainability'. Changes in resource management practice toward sustainable resource use could at least contribute to the preservation of the renewable resource base, and hence to the direct well-being of the population and to the future of the macroeconomy."

David Pearce, "The Sustainable Use of Natural Resources in Developing Countries". In R.K. Turner (ed.) *Sustainable Environmental Management* (London: Belhaven Press, 1988).

"We take development to be a vector of desirable social objectives, and elements might include:

– increases in real income per capita
– improvements in health and nutritional status
– educational achievement
– access to resources
– a 'fairer' distribution of income
– increases in basic freedoms.

. . . Sustainable development is then a situation in which the development vector increases monotonically over time."

"We summarise the necessary conditions [for sustainable development] as 'constancy of the natural capital stock'. More strictly, the requirement as for non-negative changes in the stock of natural resources such as soil and soil quality, ground surface waters and their quality, land biomass, water biomass, and the waste assimilation capacity of receiving environment."

David Pearce, Edward Barbier, Anil Markandya, *Sustainable Development and Cost-Benefit Analysis*, London Environmental Economics Centre, Paper 88-01, 1988.

"Our standard definition of sustainable development will be non-declining per capita utility – because of its self-evident appeal as a criterion for intergenerational equity."

John Pezzey, *Economic Analysis of Sustainable Growth and Sustainable Development*, World Bank, Environment Department, Working Paper No.15, Washington, DC, May 1989.

("Utility" in the context simply means "wellbeing" or "satisfaction" (eds).)

"The term 'sustainable development' suggests that the lessons of ecology can, and should, be applied to economic processes. It encompasses the ideas in the World Conservation Strategy, providing an environmental rationale through which the claims of development to improve the quality of (all) life can be challenged and tested."

Michael Redclift, *Sustainable Development* (London: Methuen, 1987).

"The core of the idea of sustainability, then, is the concept that current decisions should not impair the prospects for maintaining or improving future living standards . . . . This implies that our economic systems should be managed so that we live off the dividend of our resources, maintaining and improving the asset base. This principle also has much in common with the ideal concept of income that accountants seek to determine: the greatest amount that can be consumed in the current period without reducing prospects for consumption in the future."

"This does not mean that sustainable development demands the preservation of the current stock of natural resources or any particular mix of human, physical and natural assets. As development proceeds, the composition of the underlying asset base changes."

"There is broad agreement that pursuing policies that imperil the welfare of future generations, who are unrepresented in any political or economic forum, is unfair."

Robert Repetto, *World Enough and Time* (New Haven: Yale University Press, 1986).

"The sustainability criterion suggests that, at a minimum, future generations should be left no worse off than current generations."

"Rather than eliminating the [positive] discount rate, the present-value criterion should be complemented by other criteria, such as sustainability . . . . For example, we might choose to maximize present value subject to the constraint that future generations are not made worse off."

Tom Tietenberg, *Environmental and Natural Resource Economics* (Glenview, Ill.: Scott, Foresman and Co., 1984).

"The government espouses the concept of *sustainable* economic development.

Stable prosperity can be achieved throughout the world provided the environment is nurtured and safeguarded."

Prime Minister Margaret Thatcher, Speech to the Royal Society, 27 September 1988.

"[Sustainable development] has become an article of faith, a shibboleth: often used but little explained. Does it amount to a strategy? Does it apply only to renewable resources? What does the term actually mean? In broad terms the concept of sustainable development encompasses:

1. help for the very poor because they are left with no option other than to destroy their environment;
2. the idea of self-reliant development, within natural resource constraints;
3. the idea of cost-effective development using differing economic criteria to the traditional approach; that is to say development should not degrade environmental quality, nor should it reduce productivity in the long run;
4. the great issues of health control, appropriate technologies, food self-reliance, clean water and shelter for all;
5. the notion that people-centred initiatives are needed; human beings, in other words, are the resources in the concept."

Mustafa Tolba, *Sustainable Development – Constraints and Opportunities* (London: Butterworth, 1987).

"In principle, such an optimal [sustainable growth] policy would seek to maintain an 'acceptable' rate of growth in per-capita real incomes without depleting the national capital asset stock or the natural environmental asset stock." (p.12)

"It makes no sense to talk about the sustainable use of non-renewable resources (even with substantial recycling effort and reuse rates). Any positive rate of exploitation will eventually lead to exhaustion of the finite stock." (p.13)

" . . . in this [sustainable development] mode . . . conservation becomes the sole basis for defining a criterion with which to judge the desirability of alternative allocations of natural resources." (p.21)

R. Kerry Turner, "Sustainability, Resource Conservation and Pollution Control: an overview", in R.K. Turner (ed.), *Sustainable Environmental Management: Principles and Practice* (London: Belhaven Press, 1988).

"We came to see that a new development path was required, one that sustained human progress not just in a few places for a few years, but for the entire planet into the distant future. Thus 'sustainable development' becomes a goal not just for the 'developing' nations, but for industrial ones as well."

"Sustainable development is development that meets the needs of the present without compromising the ability of future generations to meet their own needs. It contains within it two key concepts:

– the concept of 'needs', in particular the essential needs of the world's poor, to which overriding priority should be given; and the idea of limitations imposed by the state of technology and social organisation in the environment's ability to meet present and future needs."

"Even the narrow notion of physical sustainability implies a concern for social equity between generations, a concern that must logically be extended to equity within each generation."

"Living standards that go beyond the basic minimum are sustainable only if consumption standards everywhere have regard for long-term sustainability. Yet many of us live beyond the world's ecological means, for instance in our patterns of energy use. Perceived needs are socially and culturally determined, and sustainable development requires the promotion of values that encourage consumption standards that are within the bounds of the ecological possible and to which all can reasonably aspire."

"Economic growth and development obviously involve changes in the physical ecosystem. Every ecosystem everywhere cannot be preserved intact."

"The loss [i.e. extinction] of plant and animal species can greatly limit the options of future generations; so sustainable development requires the conservation of plant and animal species."

"A pursuit of sustainable development requires . . . a production system that respects the obligation to preserve the ecological base for that development."

World Commission on Environment and Development, *Our Common Future* (London: Oxford University Press, 1987).

INDEX